THE FORGOTTEN DEAD

To Pat & Alan

With my sincere best wishes

Ken Russell

[illegible]

14 October 1994

ONE THOUSAND COPIES ONLY OF THIS SPECIAL PERSONALISED LIMITED EDITION OF THE FORGOTTEN DEAD HAVE BEEN PRINTED. THIS IS NUMBER 0857

SIGNED: Ken Russell DATE: 14 October 1994

SPECIAL LIMITED EDITION

THE FORGOTTEN DEAD

WHY 946 AMERICAN SERVICEMEN DIED OFF THE COAST OF DEVON IN 1944 – AND THE MAN WHO DISCOVERED THEIR TRUE STORY

KEN SMALL

WITH MARK ROGERSON

BLOOMSBURY

First published 1988
This special limited edition first published 1992.

Bloomsbury Publishing Limited, 2 Soho Square, London W1V 5DE

A CIP record for this book is available from the British Library.

ISBN 0 7475 1353 8

10 9 8 7 6 5 4 3 2 1

Printed in England by Clays Ltd, St Ives plc

CONTENTS

FOREWORD

In 1988 my life reached a point when everything started to go wrong. Within a few short days of returning from yet another emotional visit to the United States of America, this time to Kansas, to meet with a large number of relatives, survivors and their friends, my whole private life became a turmoil.

I struggled to find the right words for this foreword and in the end it was to be one evening, whilst watching the sun set over Slapton Sands, as it had set in 1944 on the lives of the young Americans, that the words came to express the personal feelings of heartache and emotion that have beset me for so many years. During this period many of my long-standing friends have become strangers and many strangers have now become close friends. So many people in my life just could not seem able to understand how I felt, but it was perhaps wrong of me to expect them to. The Cove Guest House, where I still live, has become for me a prison of memories, both happy and sad. However, I would like to think that I will, for some years yet, be on hand to continue meeting and talking with the countless thousands of people of all ages from all over the world who seek information regarding the disaster that hit this beautiful stretch of the South Devon coastline in 1944. So many people have taken this story and the Memorial Sherman Tank to their hearts. I have never been able to stand back after this whole crusade and take a detached look at things; I think it would have been better for my health had I been able to.

The hearts of many people throughout the world have reached out to me in so many ways. I have received written thanks from many top officials including ex-President Ronald Reagan. British premiers Margaret Thatcher and John Major have also applauded what I have done and I have received many letters from those who survived the tragedy, the relatives of those lost and well wishers. I have also heard from some of the many British Naval personnel that took part, and in particular those on "The Smokey Joe" Minesweepers who were assigned to look for wreckage but found only hundreds of bodies floating on the sea that terrible night.

I would like to thank all the many people who have helped me over the years and given me the confidence to persevere through many trials and tribulations. I would like to give special mention to the many British Veterans and their Associations who frequently hold services of remembrance at the Memorial site for their comrades who came to help us from the United States of America. To the many people who now visit Slapton Sands, I say to them, please feel welcome and enjoy the sheer beauty of the area but also never forget the young Americans who paid the supreme sacrifice in order that we may enjoy the freedom we have today.

Ken Small
May 1992

ACKNOWLEDGEMENTS

The author is grateful to the following for their assistance and involvement in helping him to create the Memorials and thus ensure that the men who died so tragically are not forgotten.

The United States of America
William H. Taft; Deputy Secretary for Defense
Robert A. Goodbary; Brigadier General U.S.A., senior military assistant to the Deputy Secretary for Defense
William L. Ball III; Secretary of the Navy
Representative Beverly B. Byron; M. C. 6th district of Maryland
R. Douglas Mathias and his wife Paula
Admiral Finkelstein (U.S.N.)
Art Humphries; Lt. Commander U.S. Navy, Commander of the U.S. European Fleet
Sally Nagata; U.S. Defense Property Disposal Service, Wiesbaden, West Germany
Melba Bowling; Department of Defense
Barbara Freudberg; Department of the Army
Judy Van Ben Thuysen; Department of the Navy
Attlee J. Wampler Jnr; Major 70th U.S. tank battalion (ret'd)
the many naval and army officers in the Pentagon, Washington D.C.
Roland Prieux; superintendent, U.S. Military cemetery, Madingley Hill, Cambridge, England
the staff of the United States embassy, London
the many relatives of those lost in Exercise Tiger and the survivors for their individual stories and accounts

Great Britain
Dean Small, Action Optics, Torcross; photo of tank on front cover
Ann Small
Tony Steer; local fisherman who started me on the right path
Sally Ann Lucas, who saw me through 5 very difficult years
Tony Seager; English Naval Involvement Research
Chris Venmore
Jim Simmons

Jim Perrot – a special thanks
Gerry Weymouth
Derek Brooking
Richard Cuming Plant Hire
David Cowley; Captain Royal Tank Regiment (ret'd)
Chris Rothwell; Corporal Royal Tank Regiment (ret'd)
John Wise of Holt, Norfolk
Fertan (Dawes Chemicals Ltd); treatment of the tank

1

THE FORGOTTEN DEAD

'I have always considered it was a wrong which should be put right, and I have worked to that end.'

The lady organist at Slapton village church had never played the national anthem of the United States before, and could we help, she wondered. Two national anthems – British and American – had to figure in the service of commemoration which was about to take place. She had come over to us to ask how it should sound. Now, it might seem a little odd that a lady organist in South Devon needed to play the American national anthem at all; still more odd that she was asking a local innkeeper and his wife for advice. But there were good reasons. We hummed the tune, and she prepared her rendition. The anthems were ready to be played.

It was Friday, 9 November 1984, and a very special service was about to take place for a very special Sherman tank. The local council had made all the necessary arrangements. Lieutenant-Colonel Tom Haase, the assistant military attaché from the US Embassy in London, was to attend, with the Bishop of Plymouth and a number of local clergy. There were quite a few local villagers, and friends of mine who had helped in what had been a long struggle to get to this moment. But it was not a massively crowded occasion because there was shortly to be another service held further up Slapton Sands, at a monument the American military had put up to thank the people of the district for evacuating their homes during World War II. It was rather ironic actually, that the other service was to commemorate the 40th anniversary of the events that led up to D-day.

There were no UK government officials and no American government officials present at the service, although an outside observer might well have concluded that there should have been. For we were to attend a commemoration in honour of men who had died in uniform, during a war. The Sherman tank was to be their memorial. I had been refused help by the Americans in setting it up. I had been offered and subsequently refused help from the British Army. But at the time I did not even think about any official English or American representation. Just to be there was sufficient.

This book is the story of the events which led up to that service, and of some of the things which have happened since. It is the story of an obsession to honour the memory of nearly 1,000 American soldiers and sailors who died needlessly in one of the great fiascos of World War II. It is also the story of the confusion and incompetence that led to such a great loss of life, of the murderous horror of one dark night off the south coast of England, and of the official indifference and deliberate concealment which dogged it for 40 years.

The fiasco was called Exercise Tiger. Over the last 17 years it has been my crusade to ensure a proper memorial for the men who lost their lives that night. I felt proud during the service of commemoration, and I still feel proud now, that at long last these men have a just memorial to their sacrifice, and that they have been given recognition for all they gave up during that period – worldwide recognition in their own country and throughout many others. I have always considered it was a wrong which should be put right and I have worked to that end. Indeed, the work is still going on, because the site of the Sherman tank has become a focal point for enquiries from relatives and friends of those who died, as well as from survivors, and I have no doubt that will go on for many years yet.

The ceremony itself that November day was very simple, very poignant and very tear-jerking. The original plan had been to hold the whole service at the tank. But the sky was heavily overcast and it was raining hard, so we moved to Slapton village church. It was appropriate really, because Slapton is in the middle of the sands. The church was full. Some people were even standing, with more outside.

I was in the front row of pews on the lefthand side of the

tiny church. Ahead of me were the archways through to the choir stalls, and all the dignitaries were seated inside that little cloister. I recall Lieutenant-Colonel Haase taking his seat, the gold braid glinting on his shoulder. I spent the whole service in tears. I suppose in the church and at the tank what I had done suddenly hit me. I had started this operation so many years before and all the pent-up emotions over the years culminated in that ceremony.

Prayers were said, and we sang 'All People that on Earth do Dwell' and 'Now Thank We All Our God'. Then the organist played the national anthems of Britain and America, and everybody moved down to the tank. A Marine bugler played the last post and I put wreaths of fresh flowers on the site. Lieutenant-Colonel Haase and George South, the chairman of South Hams Council, unveiled a plaque. It read:

> This American Sherman tank took part in the D-day practice landings at Slapton Beach in 1944 where it was lost at sea and there remained until its recovery in 1984. It stands as a memorial to those American lives lost during the course of the D-day practice landings at Slapton Beach in 1944. Their sacrifice was not in vain. Be they ever at peace.

As we walked away from the site towards the Kingfisher restaurant where we were to have a meal, I thought back over the events of the preceding decade. The whole object of my effort throughout the years had been not so much to apportion blame for this tragedy – it is too late for that. Rather, what I had sought to do was purely to bring to the attention of America, and all those interested throughout the world, the tragedy that took place on this beautiful part of the Devon coast in 1944. The more we know and understand and, most importantly, remember of the horrors of war, the less is the likelihood that those horrors will be repeated. That is also the reason I am writing this book.

It is a crusade which in many ways stems from my interest in beachcombing. Beachcombing has great fascination for me. I have found coins going back to the early fourteenth century, as well as jewellery of all kinds. But what was really to start me on the road to becoming involved in the discovery and commemoration of Exercise Tiger was that I also started to find a whole host of militaria on the beach at Slapton. I came across live shells, live bullets of all calibres, cartridge cases, shrapnel, live mines, military buttons, and men's signet rings. This indicated that something obviously pretty serious had gone on during the War in the area where I now lived.

I knew of a monument which existed along the main road at Slapton Sands, less than a mile from the guesthouse I ran with my wife in Torcross. It was erected in 1954 by the American Government and on it was an inscription thanking the local people of five villages all round this area, including Torcross, who had to vacate their homes and their farms and their lands in late 1943 to make way for what was to be a practice exercise for the landings on Utah Beach on 6 June, D-day, in 1944.

My curiosity was aroused and asking around I discovered that many Americans had lost their lives here. I did not at first know how many, information was very scanty, but figures were put at anywhere between 500 and 1000 men. My investigations uncovered the fact that the exercise which took place had used live ammunition and was based around Slapton Sands, which was chosen because of its likeness to Utah Beach. It involved some 30,000 men of the US Army and the US Navy, plus small contingents of the Britsh Navy, in what was to amount almost to a full-scale rehearsal for D-day. Exercise Tiger, as it was known, took place in April 1944. It was a major undertaking and a tragic one.

In the early 1970s, after I had begun to find all the militaria on the beach, a local fisherman friend of mine told me about an object some three-quarters of a mile out to sea in 60 feet of water, on which trawlers had been snagging their nets for many years. He suggested that he and I went along with a couple of divers to investigate this 'wreck' or whatever it was.

When the divers went down they discovered nothing less than a complete Sherman tank. They even brought up two propellers from it, for as it turned out this was a special version of the tank adapted for travelling through water. As we came ashore, still thrilled with our discovery, I thought that if I could purchase and recover that tank it would be a most fitting memorial for those men who had lost their lives here, and also for the survivors of the exercise and their families. I spent many hours planning it and seeking advice from as many sources as possible. Then in 1984 which was the 40th anniversary of D-day I decided that this would be the appropriate time to raise it if ever it was going to be raised.

Since the recovery of the tank and the dedication, I have received literally hundreds of letters from all over America containing graphic accounts of what went on during the night of Exercise Tiger. Many have tales of horror – and heroism – to tell, from the soldier who saved many lives by shooting through a hawser which was preventing a life raft from being launched, to the collision between two tanks – supposedly modified for waterborne landings – one of which was to be raised from the seabed 40 years later.

It is an ironic fact that while almost 1000 men lost their lives at Slapton, only some 200 were killed during the actual landing at Utah Beach. Exercise Tiger was kept highly secret at the time; it had to be. People have said it was a cover up. I am not so sure that a cover up – with all its Watergate connotations – is quite the right word. But what did happen was that it was forgotten; it was not spoken about. At the time, the men who survived were threatened with court martial if they even discussed the exercise with the doctors who were treating them, let alone anyone else. So great were the restraints placed upon them that some still feel unable to talk about it now, more than 40 years after the event. But a great number have talked and written about it to me.

During my trips to the Pentagon and my phone calls, I have also obtained a complete dossier of the official records of the exercise. I have seen film of the exercise taken at the time. I have accident reports, damage reports, burial reports, injury diagnoses and facts as to the whereabouts of the men. A lot were buried in very shallow graves near Slapton at the time, then later disinterred and reburied – initially at Brookwood in Surrey and then at the American cemetery on Madingley Hill, near Cambridge.

In my investigations, I also have discovered that apart from the American presence in the operation, some 32 English naval vessels were involved, ranging from heavy cruisers downwards, shelling and pounding the shore. As one man who served on the cruiser HMS *Hawkins* described their shelling of Slapton, 'We created hell on shore'.

This book tells the story of Exercise Tiger and its aftermath not from the point of view of the military historian, or the retired commander, but in the words of the soldiers who were there on the night, and of an Englishman for whom their proper recognition has become a lifetime's work.

The story of Exercise Tiger really starts with the evacuation of the South Hams – the civilian exercise which is remembered in that other memorial further along the beach at Slapton from my Sherman tank.

Once the landing beaches on the French coast had been selected, it was essential that stretches of coastline in Britain with similar features be made available for training. General Montgomery, the land force commander for Overlord, had already used the South Hams area of Devon for a military landing exercise in 1938 on Slapton Sands. Ten miles inland lay Dartmoor and the established training areas already used by the Army. With the outbreak of war the area, like much of Britain's coastline with vulnerable landing beaches, had already been shut off to the public and fortified with mines and barbed wire. One of the most famous local landmarks, the Royal Sands Hotel, an isolated building right on the seafront at Slapton, had been evacuated in 1939 and closed 'for the duration'. But a local farmer's dog named Pincher later set off a mine buried close by, killing himself and demolishing part of the building in the process, thus giving the beach area an already war-torn look. Now the military hierarchy decided that not only the existing training and defence areas, but a considerably larger area of land would need to be requisitioned if the D-day rehearsals were to be conducted in sufficient secrecy and with sufficient accuracy.

So it was that, on 4 November 1943, the chairman of the Devon County Council, Sir John Daw, received a telephone call from the War Office informing him that a considerable part of the land under his authority was being requisitioned under the 1939 Defence Regulations and Compensation Act and had to be totally evacuated by 20 December. The regional commissioner, Sir Hugh Elles, who had the responsibility in the southwest of England for co-ordinating any large-scale civilian movements in wartime immediately called all the relevant parties together for briefings to be held at the castle in Exeter. The first was attended by the local authoritics concerned, including the voluntary organisations, who were told of the scope of the evacuation. They were advised that the Royal Navy would provide men to assist with the setting up of special information centres, and that the Navy would provide a hostel for billeting the army of officials who would be necessary to mastermind the move. Many of the details of these preparations for the evacuation, and the evacuation itself, were recorded by Grace Bradbeer, a WVS driver at the time, who wrote an account of the move called 'The Land Changed its Face'.

The second planning meeting was composed of clergy who served the neighbourhood due to be evacuated. They heard the astounding news that a total evacuation of 30,000 acres was to take place at once, involving parts of six parishes, 3,000 people, 180 farms, village shops and other dwellings, affecting 750 families in all. The area involved consisted of a triangle from Torcross to Blackpool Sands and stretching uphill to Blackawton at its apex. It included the villages of Torcross, Slapton, Strete, Blackawton, East Allington, Sherford, Stokenham and Chillington, All farm possessions, animals, agricultural machinery, household goods, indeed anything movable of any value, and as many crops still in the ground as could be saved, were all to be taken away. This whole enormous task had to be completed in six weeks. The clergy were also informed that the government promised to pay every expense in connection with the evacuation, would give all help in finding temporary accommodation, would pay rents, grant free storage during the period of absence, and that everything would be brought back under the same guarantee while any damage would be repaired and paid for. Finally, they were told that it would be necessary to start the scheme at once for the land was due to be handed over to the War Office on 20 December for troop-training. They were asked at present to use their discretion as to whom they passed on this information, as the parishes in question were to be informed officially at special meetings within a few days.

The occupation was to last for about six months, but it was pointed out that the inhabitants might not be able to return at once since a clearing-up operation would almost certainly be necessary. But because of the value of the agricultural land involved, the greatest efforts would be made to reinstate the farmers as soon as possible.

Word began to leak out. A gang of boys up in the village of Torcross was playing around one evening, when some of the older men came in from work and the word went round the village that an evacuation was going to take place. To the boys it sounded like a new kind of game, but the old men said it was impossible and could never happen, because it was too big an undertaking to clear every farm and every person. The rumours continued to spread, and were confirmed by some army officers who were billeted in the village. But still everyone said it would just not be possible to clear the area in time. Then, a couple of days later, it was made official: everybody had to go – farmers, cattle, everything.

It was on 12 November – a day after the memorial services for the Armistice of World War I – that the Lord Lieutenant of Devon addressed a meeting held at East Allington church to explain the position to the people, namely that this particular part of the South Hams was to be used for practice for assault landings before a Second Front was opened. Later in the day he held another meeting at Stokenham church. The next day Sir John Daw held similar meetings at Blackawton church and at Slapton village hall and the news was received in the same shocked fashion. It was difficult for some to believe the shattering news, for the area was richly agricultural and the need for home-grown food greater than ever. Many were at a loss to understand why such valuable land should be especially commandeered. It had to be explained to them over and over again, that it would be criminal to send troops to land in enemy occupied country as front line men without giving them some experience of what to expect. For many in the South

Hams, that was all they would ever really know. Fleets of lorries were commandeered, accommodation arranged for the 'evacuees', crops left in the ground. Within a few weeks the whole area became a collection of ghost villages.

It was a terrible time for some. One man committed suicide rather than leave – he was in his seventies, and he said that if he was to leave Slapton it would be in a box. Everyone was very shocked, and not least by the limited amount of time allowed. They were told that they had to be out by 20 December. An old neighbour of mine, Arthur Bowls, told me that people had to leave cats and dogs, even guinea fowl behind, as nobody could catch them. The Bowls family took two geese with them for Christmas. They had the geese in a box, one for Christmas and one for New Year, but when they came to take them out and as Arthur grabbed one, the other one flew off and set out along the line of the river. They never saw it again. It was particularly hard for the farmers. They had to sell their animals at a time when nobody wanted them, and they had a lot to sell. Everybody was in the same boat. They had to try and take them to the markets gradually and sell them off. But in desperation they also had to slaughter some. It certainly did not help the price that everyone was trying to sell at the same time.

The older people never used to leave the village, so it was very frightening for them to get six weeks' notice to leave. Herman and Kathleen Blank were just two among those evacuated. Kathleen's mother was very ill when they were moved out of Slapton, so an ambulance had to be sent to move her. Then they were told to put their furniture out on a particular morning, and it would be collected and moved for them. But the lorry did not arrive and it was not collected. So they had to take it all back into the house and put it out again the next day. Kathleen's father did not drive a car, so she had to drive herself. They went first to her cousin at Totnes. He looked across the valley and said there was a farm on the other side of the valley, and he would take them over and see if they could get help. So they went over and found a place to stay. It was an oldish couple, who took Kathleen's parents in, but after six months they had to move yet again because the people wanted them out of the farmhouse and they ended the war in a bungalow in Totnes.

Les Tabb, another of my neighbours, told me that he was working on a farm. His family managed to get a place because they had a brother out of the area, but they still had to sell some of their cattle as well. His mother and father went to Dartmouth and worked on a farm there. On the day, the Admiralty organised everything. Men even came and helped to cut out and tie up all the straw and hay for the cattle. The villagers did not really blame the Americans for what was happening at the time – indeed they did not really connect it with the Americans at all. To them, it was all the work of the Admiralty. They moved out thinking it would only be for six months, and for some it turned out to be 11 months.

Once they had moved away, it became very difficult to find out what was happening in the area. The boundaries were patrolled and all civilians were barred. What they did know was that a great deal of ammunition was being expended in whatever exercises were taking place. Some of those further up the coast could see boats coming in and out of the bay and, on occasion, shells being fired ashore. A rumour went round that a group of soldiers was killed sheltering from a live ammunition barrage under the bridge across Slapton Ley; others were said to have been killed taking shelter in a barn.

It was only when they came back that they started to realise how much damage had been caused, and how devastating the exercises had been. One old chap who lived near Les Tabb used to be a gamekeeper. Everyone knew him as Kedeper Dean, and he moved back onto his farm about two months before the rest of the community. He went back to collect and catch rabbits – partly for food, and partly because the area was becoming overrun with them. He said when he first came back there was no electricity and no water and he was forced to rely on oil lamps.

All the houses were damaged, some much more than others. One family had a number of big cupboards in their farmhouse, but all the drawers had been removed and burned in the fire. Half of them were still there, charred and useless. All their gardens and fields had run to seed and roots. Driving across a field in a tractor afterwards was almost impossible because there were so many shell craters. They could not count the shell holes, they were so close packed together and the number seemed to run into thousands. They also found thousands of rounds of live ammunition, some of it still unwrapped in cardboard boxes. The soldiers were suppposed to have gone over the ground and removed everything dangerous, but that turned out to be far from the case. The villagers found ammunition everywhere – even stuffed into rabbit holes. It was very lucky that no children were killed because cases of bullets, shells and mortar bombs were constantly being turned up. The police would call the bomb disposal people to clear them, and a few days later still more would be found. It went on for years.

One day a group of men was repairing some of the hedges. They looked under the hedgerow and saw a box containing brand new mortar shells. They took them out of the box, intending to dispose of them, but for reasons best known to himself Les Tabb's father decided to throw them onto a bonfire they were making. There was a series of loud bangs and one flew off towards the beach, another went into an old ash tree and set the hedge on fire, and another went off towards their house. It was their good fortune that the hay ricks did not catch fire.

As for their houses, squads of workmen were drafted in to repair them – the Admiralty paid for it all, but even so there were problems. One elderly lady told me that all properties were valued by the Admiralty, even cracks in the ceiling were noted before the evacuation. But when the officials came round afterwards, even if the crack was very much worse, they would say that it was cracked before they left. When they were evacuated, nothing was too much trouble, but when they came back it was very different. Nor was the compensation enough. Many of the farmworkers did not own their property so the money went to the landlords. True they let their tenants off some of the rent but it was not enough. Indeed, many families never came back, they stayed on the farms to which they had been evacuated – they did not really have homes to come back to.

But what had been going on all this time? What had caused such widespread destruction? And what were the stories of men being killed? In fact, the evacuation completed, the South Hams was occupied by 30,000 US troops who camped in and around the deserted villages, and prepared for intensive rehearsals for the invasion landings. Their prime site of interest was Slapton Sands, not just because of its already battered appearance, but most importantly because it was a stretch of coast that closely resembled the area of Normandy coast code-named Utah Beach.

Slapton and its surrounding area became the focus for intensive military activity, with the establishment of observation and defence posts, roadblocks, gun emplacements and fortifications. Roads were straightened, gates removed, gardens trampled down. As I said, all local people apart from civil defence officials were barred, and the US troops were banned from talking to outsiders. Secrecy and suspicion dominated the coast. The troops' purpose became a little clearer to the locals when stories started to leak out of nighttime explosions and seaborne activity, not that they knew the code-words or the details, of course. Because this was the series of landings which would lead up to Exercise Tiger, the main rehearsal for the Utah Beach landings, set for 27 April.

2

EXERCISE TIGER

'At a few minutes past two, a terrific explosion was heard from astern, and the LST 507 was seen to burst into flames.'

It had been a meeting of the heads of the Allied Governments at Casablanca in January 1943 which set in motion the final planning for the launch of Operation Overlord – the D-day landings in France – on 6 June 1944. That planning would include the training and preparation of an Allied army of three and a half million men, including one and a half million Americans. Transport would be provided by a fleet of more than 1,200 warships, guarding 4,000 landing craft and 1,600 merchant and ancillary vessels, and supported by 11,500 aircraft and 3,500 gliders.

As far as the South Hams was concerned, training exercises actually began with the United States V Army Corps practising on 15 December 1943 in Start Bay, and in the nearby Torbay. Slapton's unspoiled beach of coarse red gravel, fronting a shallow lagoon, and backed by grassy bluffs impressed all the senior officers with its likeness to what they called the 'Far Shore'. The training schedule was long and designed to be thorough, but it was greatly complicated by the progressive arrival in England of gunfire support ships and small craft with very inexperienced crews. Harry C Butcher, one of Eisenhower's aides, wrote in his memoirs:

> I am concerned over the absence of toughness and alertness of young American officers whom I saw on this trip. They seem to regard the war as one grand manoeuvre in which they are having a happy time. Many seem as green as growing corn. How will they act in battle and how will they look in three months time?

> A good many of the full colonels also give me a pain. They are fat, grey, and oldish. Most of them wear the Rainbow Ribbon of the last war and are still fighting it. The lst US Division is the only experienced American infantry division actually in the assault, although the 9th, which also was in Africa, is in the close follow-up.
>
> On the Navy's side, our crews also are green, but they seem to know how to handle their boats, yet when I dictate this, I recall that in plain daylight, with a smooth sea with our LCI standing still, she nearly had her stern carried away by a landing craft fitted out as an anti-aircraft ship. We were missed only by inches – in clear daylight.

The intention was to simulate the real landings in full. Landing craft would attempt to land invading troops on the shore, while naval and land batteries and forces would try to repel them. The first landings had been code-named Operation Duck. Next, towards the end of March 1944 came Operation Beaver, to be followed in April by Operation Tiger. Because of the concerns about the battle hardness of the officers and troops it was decided to use live ammunition, fired over the heads and in front of the invading troops. This decision, taken by General Eisenhower, Supreme Allied Commander, was communicated to senior level officers, but not to all the troops.

The key to the success of the operations was to be thorough and effective communications between the 'defenders' and 'invaders' – and this was the first crucial breakdown. The carefully prepared network of radio frequencies for commanding officers on shore, inland and on ship was issued with vital errors caused by typing mistakes in the frequency numbers.

These errors caused a major failure in communications, and in the process demolished the all-important timing between the various participating units. The authenticity required by Eisenhower and his advisers became grotesquely real as casualties mounted. Troops in the landing craft who had assumed the exercise was another 'dry run' became confused and panic-stricken as the live ammunition started causing genuine deaths and injuries. Many of those who took part in the early exercises remember the shock of young soldiers seeing comrades killed and wounded as the 'warring' factions fired on each other at random, often not realising their ammunition was live, as the planned sequences of the practice went haywire without the vital radio communications.

All the same, the relentless schedule of training had to continue, as D-day was by this time firmly set for 6 June. I have obtained a copy of the actual document which set out the way in which Tiger – the next landing rehearsal in the sequence – was to be conducted:

Supreme Headquarters
Allied Expeditionary Force
G-3 Division

19 April 1944

Subject: Exercise Tiger

1. Exercise Tiger will involve the concentration, marshalling and embarkation of troops in the Torbay – Plymouth area, and a short movement by sea under the control of the US Navy, disembarkation with Naval and Air support at Slapton Sands, a beach assault using service ammunition, the securing of a beachhead and a rapid advance inland.
2. Major troop units are the VII Corps Troops, 4th infantry Division, the l0lst and 52nd Airborne Divisions, lst Engineer Special Brigade, Force 'U' and supporting Air Force units.
3. During the period H-60 to H-45 minutes, fighter-bombers attack inland targets on call from the l0lst AB Division and medium bombers attack three targets along the beach. Additional targets will be bombed by both fighter-bombers and medium bombers on call from ground units. Simulated missions will also be flown with the target areas marked by smoke pots.
4. Naval vessels fire upon beach obstacles from H-50 to H-hour. Smoke may be used during the latter part of the

naval bombardment both from naval craft by 4.2 chemical mortars and at H-hour by planes, if weather conditions are favourable. Naval fire ceases at H-hour.

5. The schedule of the exercise is as follows:

22 April - Move to marshalling area commences.

D-day 27 April – 101st AB Div simulates landing. Preparatory bombardment by air and navy. Assault landing and advance of 4th Div.

28-29 April - Advance of 4th Div. & 101st AB Div continues. 82nd AB Div. simulates landing, secures and holds objective.

(Exercise terminates on 29 April)

TOP SECRET

Force 'U', for Utah Beach, was under the command of Rear Admiral Don P Moon, US Navy, and his troops and equipment were to be embarked in the same ships and for the most part in the same ports whence it was planned that they would leave for France a few months later. During the night of 26/27 April they proceeded through Lyme Bay and out on a long, looping course, to give the impression of the time it would take actually to travel over to France. There were minecraft sweeping ahead of them as if crossing the Channel. As German E-boats sometimes prowled the Channel on favourable nights, the commander in chief in Plymouth, who was responsible for protecting the rehearsal, placed extra patrols across the mouth of Lyme Bay, consisting of two destroyers, three MTB – motor torpedo boats – and two motor gunboats. Another MTB patrol was laid on to watch Cherbourg.

Following the 'bombardment' on Slapton Sands, the first landings were made during the morning of 27 April and unloading continued throughout that day and the next, when the follow-up convoy of another eight LSTs – or Landing Ship Tanks – was expected. It would be this follow-up convoy which would meet with death and destruction on a scale they could not have imagined as they set out from port.

Although there were a number of British ships stationed off the south coast, including those facing Cherbourg, only two vessels were assigned to accompany the follow-up convoy – a corvette, HMS *Azalea*, and a World War I destroyer, HMS *Scimitar*. But after being damaged in a minor collision, the destroyer put into port and a replacement vessel came to the scene too late. This was one of the most critical errors of Exercise Tiger

But that was not the only mistake. Because of a typographical error in orders, the US LSTs were on a radio frequency different from the corvette and the British naval headquarters ashore. When one of the British ships spotted some German torpedo boats soon after midnight, a report quickly reached the British corvette but not the LSTs. Assuming that the US vessels had received the same report as he had, the commander of the corvette made no effort to alert them. So it was that the German E-boats had a clear run to attack the lightly defended convoy. The military details of the night are documented in the Action Reports of the various LST commanders. From a source inside the Pentagon, I have obtained a complete set of the Action Reports, from which it is possible to make a minute-by-minute reconstruction of the part played in Exercise Tiger by the follow-up convoy, codenamed 'T-4'.

In overall charge of the LST Group was Commander B J Skahill, in the lead ship, the LST 515. It was on 3 May 1944 that he submitted his report of what happened during Exercise Tiger, along with separate reports from each of the commanders of the other LSTs. It is worth remembering that an LST was an ocean-going vessel, capable of carrying several hundred men, lorries and tanks. It was not just a flat-bottomed landing craft to bring a few men onto a beach, but a major assault ship weighing some four and a half thousand tons. To manoeuvre one at night under attack from much smaller and lighter craft, would have been no easy task.

LST Group 32 left Plymouth at 9:45 am on 27 April with the Plymouth section of Convoy T-4 composed of the LSTs 515, 496, 531, and 58 (the LST 58 was towing two pontoon causeways). The Plymouth section proceeded almost due south to a point near the Eddystone Rocks, where it was joined by the escort vessel, HMS *Azalea*, and then tracked east and northeast along the coast to a point off Brixham where it was joined by the Brixham section of Convoy T-4 composed of the LSTs 499, 289 and 507.

The convoy was proceeding in one column at a speed of five knots and stayed in the order 515, 496, 511, 531, 58, 499, 289, and 507, with each LST about 400 yards behind the next.

During the night, wrote Commander Skahill, commencing about half an hour after midnight, they saw various white and yellow flares of undetermined origin and significance. The number they observed at any one time, in any one locality, varied from one to five. Some appeared to be a rocket–type flare, others parachute–flares with elevations from 10 degrees to 25 degrees and separated by periods of five seconds to 30 seconds. At no time during the night did they hear or see any aircraft – friendly or otherwise.

Then, at about 1:30 am on 28 April, gunfire broke out astern. Everyone went to their stations. They did not realise it at the time, but they were being attacked by a formation of nine German E-boats form Cherbourg, which had slipped past the patrols without being recognised. These were a formidable foe.

A German E-boat was a fast moving hunter-killer. By the Allies, they were called 'E' for enemy, by the Germans 'S–boote', 'schnell' or fast boats. Each was armed with either two torpedo tubes and four torpedoes or two torpedoes and up to five mines. In addition they carried three 20mm guns and one 40mm gun. The E-boats were about 35 metres long, grey and slim. They could travel at speeds of up to 40 knots, and had a range of some 700 miles.

Crew quarters on E-boats were very limited in space. Everything was stripped down to make them fast and light. Total crew at the beginning of the war was about 28, but this was later increased due to extra armament to between 32 and 34. Only about half the men actually had bunks to sleep in, the others used hammocks, or slept on or under tables in the wireless room, as well as among the torpedo tubes. A very small galley allowed them to prepare hot meals and coffee. Indeed so tight was space that normally they had quarters ashore and went on board only for maintenance work and operations at sea.

On the night of Exercise Tiger, Oberleutnant zur See Günther Rabe was commanding officer in S-130, which belonged to the 9th Flotilla and had been based at Cherbourg since the middle of February 1944 in order to reinforce the German anti-invasion forces. Rabe was 26 years old at the time, and has since passed on to me his memories of that engagement.

During the night of 27/28 April the 5th and 9th E-boat-Flotilla were ordered by the Führer der Schnellboote (officer in charge of E-boats) to carry out a normal reconnaissance mission from their base at Cherbourg into the Lyme Bay area. Rabe does not remember if they had any particular information about ship movements in the area. They knew, however, that during April 1944 there was constant traffic on the coastal route off the south coast of England, as they met with increasing resistance from a rapidly growing number of gunboats, launches and other escorts. Despite the British defenders, however, they were building up a high score of 'kills' among the transports rehearsing for D-day, although the Germans of course had no idea from where or when the invasion was actually to come.

That night, after leaving the port of Cherbourg at a few minutes past 10 pm, they turned west, passed the island of Alderney and the rocks of the Casquets, and then turned up to the northwest and made a course towards Lyme Bay. They encountered no British destroyers or gunboats off Cherbourg, which they might have expected to do, since the British had a defensive screen around the area to cover just this sort of eventuality. The 9th flotilla with four boats held the westerly positions, whilst the 5th flotilla with five boats was to head for the eastern part of the Bay. They reached the usual Channel convoy route without any sign of a convoy or ship, nor any contact with covering forces. They crossed the route and set off for the inner part of Lyme Bay, later on turning northeast to east on a nearly parallel course to continue their search. Rabe remembers that there were flares in a southeasterly direction, which he assumed were fired from escorts to illuminate the boats from the 5th flotilla.

Then suddenly they found themselves in visual contact with

the convoy of LSTs, lined up, they thought, in a rather long formation. From their position to the south and east of the LSTs, they could not see any escorts, so they approached to a good range at comparatively high speed in order to come to a favourable position for torpedo attack.

From his notes, Rabe knows that his boat fired two torpedoes at about 2:5. As he later found out, S-143 launched her torpedos against the same LST a few seconds later. A definite hit was observed. Shortly after they saw fire on board the LST and a dense cloud of smoke rose from the ship. The actual sinking was not seen, as by then the S-130 had turned away for a short leg towards the west and thereafter to the south. Conscious of the fact that there were many more ships in the area they felt they could not attempt to close in to look for survivors.

Let us take up the story now from the American point of view. The LST 496 was second in line in the convoy, immediately behind the ship with the commander on board. Shortly after 1:30, LST 507 was observed firing anti-surface from her starboard battery. 'Action stations' was called but the ship was unable to pick up any target on radar. At just before 2 am they changed course to come round in a loop and head back in towards the shore. It was here that the E-boats made their visual contact. The 496 was simply following in the wake of the 515. Then LST 507 was torpedoed. The front part of the convoy maintained course and speed. A few minutes later the men on the 496 saw an unidentified LST behind them open fire with her starboard battery at a target about 90 degrees from her. Fire was returned from low in the water with blue tracer. As the convoy continued on course, LSTs 289 and 531 were torpedoed within a few seconds of each other. Now the 496 broke formation. They made a 90 degree turn to port, went ahead at flank speed and gave the order to open fire with their after battery on a radar target that had been picked up at a distance of about one and one-quarter miles. But they hit nothing. The commander gave the order to cease fire and commenced zigzagging, endeavouring to present the ship's stern to the radar targets. But the attackers by that time had moved on.

LST 511 had what was probably the best view of the attacking boats of any of the Americans, though they had little more success in defending the convoy. They were third in line behind the leader, and when LSTs 515 and 496 commenced firing on their unidentified target three of the 511's 20mm guns and one 40mm commenced firing on the same target. They were immediately silenced by the order 'cease firing', as the target had disappeared as quickly as it had come. The guns on the 511 did not fire again during the action, but that was far from the end of the matter for the men on board. As soon as they commenced firing, the after port guns on LST 496 strafed their decks wounding numerous navy personnel. Their range was no more than the 400 yards separation between the ships. In a fairly charitable comment, the action report of the 511 notes that the 496 'may have been trying to fire at an E-boat reported by four witnesses to have passed.' Certainly the 511 was also hit by German fire, a fact verified by several bullet holes which slanted upward, and could be explained in no other manner. Although it seemed like longer to many of those on board, the entire firing of all ships concerned in this part of the action lasted no more than about two minutes.

The E-boat passed at approximately 40 knots according to American calculations, which meant that it was travelling at full speed. It passed close in, right below their bows. The first they heard was the noise of the motors, which was initially reported to be an aeroplane, as it sounded much like one. The sound, though loud, had a muffled quality. The boat approached on a course heading from port to starboard, passing directly in front of the ship by no more than 15 yards, but at this point none of the guns on the 511 was able to depress sufficiently to fire on it. The boat then made two sharp turns, first 90 degrees to starboard, then back to its original course to port. It then disappeared from view. No reliable description of the craft could be given due to the darkness of the night and its colouring – only the wake end and its gunfire were seen. It had commenced firing when slightly off the 511's port bow and continued until lost from sight to starboard.

The men on the 511 may have been strafed by their own comrades, and by an E-boat, but in relative terms they were lucky. While the ships at the front of the convoy were observing what was happening, and for quite some time keeping in formation, those further back were under much heavier attack. On board LST 499, the first sign of anything unusual was at about 1:20, when they felt a vibration like that of a nearby depth charge. A few seconds later the same sensation repeated itself. Just prior to the second vibration LST 507, the last in line, was seen to veer to port.

Then an unidentified craft opened fire on the convoy from astern and action stations was sounded. Red and green tracers passed overhead at about mast height, landing all around the ship. The gunfire seemed to originate from an invisible craft on their starboard quarter. The tracers seemed to be spent because of their 'dropping off' effect or trajectory, indicating to the men on the 499 that the invisible craft was firing from some distance. This gunfire lasted for about four minutes, and after it ceased the LST 289 moved up to within 300 yards of the stern of the 499 and the LST 507 returned to station. Twenty minutes passed without further disturbance and, because they received no instructions, they assumed the gunfire to have been a part of the exercise. They could not have been more wrong.

At a few minutes past two, a terrific explosion was heard from astern and the LST 507 burst into flames. About the same time they saw the wake of a torpedo abeam the 499 to starboard, and about 100 to 150 feet distant. The wake made about a 45 degree angle with their heading. They immediately gave full left rudder and all engines ahead full. The bow lookout reported that the torpedo wake cleared the bow by no more than 20 feet. They turned on their radar immediately after the LST 507 was torpedoed, but were unable to pick up any suspicious vessels.

There were now a series of confused course changes. At the same time that the 499 gave full left rudder the LST 289 also veered to port. They steered various courses until they were parallel with the LST 58. In other words, the convoy was bunching up at the centre. At just after 2:10, they throttled back to standard speed and then to one-third speed. During all this time they were expecting instructions from the convoy leader or from the escort ship, but they received none. They did not know whether to stay in formation, scatter, or make for shore.

At 2:20, there was another explosion and the LST 531 burst into flames, taking an immediate list to starboard. About a minute before this torpedoing, the LST 531 had been fired upon and she immediately returned the fire and firing between both the LST 531 and the invisible craft continued for a few seconds after the torpedoing. Then a second explosion was heard during this exchange of gunfire and the stern of the LST 531 burst into flames. The 499 again veered sharply to port and changed to full speed ahead. At the same time all the ships scattered.

Just after the second explosion a long, slender, light grey craft, moving at high speed, was seen to the starboard of the LST 531 at an estimated distance of two miles by the officer in charge of the bow guns, the bow lookout, and the No. 3 gun crew. It might have been the convoy escort, they thought. More likely what they saw was an E-boat.

At 2:25 the LST 499 radioed a distress message on the 490 kilocycle wavelength. It was, 'SSSS SSSS SSSS 3WYX V 3PQP 2800240 BT SUBMARINE ATTACK BT 2800240'. The signal would be picked up, and relief ships sent out, but they would arrive too late to do anything other than pick up those few survivors still alive after a long night in the water.

The 499 was not directly attacked, but further along the line of the convoy, other LSTs were clearly being hit. It was at 2:4 that LST 507 was struck. All electric power failed, the craft burst into flames, the fire got out of control and the survivors were forced to abandon ship. One of those on board LST 507 was Lieutenant J S Murdock. He reported afterwards that at approximately 1:45 they had heard gunfire and observed tracers apparently coming from their port quarter.

'Action stations' was sounded, but they could not work out the source of the firing. They heard intermittent firing between the time of the first shots and the moment when the ship was torpedoed on the starboard side. The torpedo actually struck the auxilliary engine room and all electric power failed immediately. The main engines stopped and the ship burst into flames. Fire-fighting was attempted by the crew but nearly all of their equipment was either inoperative, due to power failure, or inaccessible due to fire. What fire-fighting equipment was available was used, but it was inadequate. The fire gained headway relentlessly.

At some time around 2:45 on the morning of 28 April, Lieutenant Murdock abandoned ship with the then commanding officer, Lieutenant J S Swarts. They had given the order to abandon ship 10 minutes previously and stayed on board to ensure an orderly evacuation. As Murdock put it later: 'As far as could be observed the abandoning of the ship was orderly. The opportunity was afforded only to launch two lifeboats and at least two life rafts.' Survivors of the LST 507 have related the grim events of abandoning ship and struggling in the water in some detail.

It was not until almost 5 am that the LST 515 arrived on the scene, lowered boats and engaged in picking up survivors. Murdock was on a raft which went alongside the LST 515 and he was hoisted aboard. The official statistics for the LST 507 were as follows. Originally aboard, Navy – 165; Army – 282. Navy: 47 dead and 24 missing. Army: 131 dead and missing.

A few minutes after the 507 came under attack, LST 531 was hit by two torpedoes, burst into flames, and within six minutes had rolled over and sunk.

Ensign Douglas Harlander was the senior survivor on LST 531, and he compiled the report of what happened. 'Action stations' was sounded shortly after 1:30, as elsewhere in the convoy. When Harlander got to the bridge he was informed that gunfire was heard and tracers had been seen, though he himself did not see the tracers nor hear any gunfire. He was told that the gunfire was from the direction of their stern but was not directed at his ship and that the firing had not lasted over one minute. Then a ship was reported on fire in the distance off their starboard quarter. Ensign Cantrell, who saw the ship, and Ensign Harlander both observed the fire and were puzzled as to its identity. It was in fact the burning 507. Just about the time they realised it was an LST, their own ship was torpedoed on the starboard side by two torpedoes separated by about one minute. The first torpedo hit squarely amidships, the second in the vicinity of number three lifeboat. The ship immediately burst into flames and their 40mm gun commenced firing to starboard. All electric power failed, the telephones were inoperative, and the engines stopped. Fire-fighting was attempted but was futile, as all the apparatus they tried to use failed to function. It was quickly apparent to those on board that the fire could not be controlled and they tried to release one of the remaining lifeboats. These efforts were no more successful than the fire-fighting, due to the intense heat, while two further lifeboats had been demolished by the initial explosions.

Shortly afterwards, the ship rolled over and Harlander gave the command to abandon ship; he estimated that not more than 15 men were in his vicinity at the time; many of the soldiers and sailors had already jumped overboard. There were 142 Navy and 354 Army personnel on board the LST 531 when she set out. Totals of dead and missing were 114 Navy and 310 Army. It was not until 7 am that morning that the Navy survivors were picked up.

The last ship to come under attack that night was the LST 289. She had sighted an E-boat at just before 2:30 and opened fire. The E-boat retaliated with a torpedo hit. A number of men were killed, but the LST managed to make port under her own power.

Harry Mettler was commanding officer of LST 289. Like many of the others he had experienced 'bumps' or shocks near the boat, but the first clear indication of an enemy attack was when he saw the tracer being fired at the 507 about 600 yards astern of them. He was in the super con – or control room – at the time. In the opinion of Mettler and his gunnery officer it appeared to be 40mm gunfire from 2500 to 4000 yards distance, and coming from almost due west, but at no time did anyone see the craft firing, even though the fire came almost directly down the path of the moon, which was then very low in the sky. The 507 sheered to their port and came ahead nearly abeam of them. The enemy fire was then diverted to the 289 from dead astern, most of it being well over the ship. But at no time were any flashes observed, making it futile for them to return the fire, and only serving to give away their own position.

The 289's gun stations were put on local control with instructions to open fire only if an enemy craft was in view. When they were attacked, they were manning one bow and one stern 40mm gun, after which they immediately went on action stations. The firing lasted about 10 minutes and they received no hits out of 200 to 300 rounds fired. Shortly after the firing ceased, the 507 came back into formation about 700 yards astern of them. Like those on the LST 499, they started to wonder whether the firing might after all have just been a part of the exercise. Then there was an explosion amidships on the starboard side of the 507, with a great flash of flames which seemed to spread instantly from stem to stern. The middle part of the convoy broke formation. The 499 pulled up on the port side of the 58 and the 289 sheered to port.

Aware both of the full load of Army personnel for whom they were primarily responsible and of their own vulnerability, the officers on the 289 considered it unwise to go to the assistance of the 507.

By this time, the entire convoy was out of formation and when the next ship exploded they were unable to identify it. They were by then running at almost full speed using right and left full rudder at four or five minute intervals to make an evasive pattern. It was later reported by several gun crews that a torpedo wake passed astern off their starboard quarter and another across their port bow. Their erratic course had clearly achieved its goal. Just before 2:30, four port 40mm guns and three 20mm guns opened fire at what some gun crews described as a fast white boat similar to the British M1 series, while others were firing at a torpedo wake which was headed for a point one fourth of the way forward of the stern. The torpedo was approximately 100 yards away from the ship when the officers in the super con saw it. They had to move very quickly. The order had just been given for left full rudder, but as the ship was still swinging fast to the right the prior order was belayed and the rudder returned to full right. The torpedo appeared to be going at not more than 15 or 20 knots and from the super con it seemed at first that it was going to miss. But it hit the ship near the stern. It exploded with considerable flash and roar, but did not shake the ship noticeably – only a few light bulbs had broken filaments and there were no injuries. Fortunately, it struck sufficiently high that the screws themselves were not damaged.

Fire broke out in the crew quarters and on the navigation bridge, but the fire hoses were brought from amidships and the fire was put out before gaining any headway. With their electrics still intact they were in a much better position to fight the fire than those on the other two crippled ships. One steward's mate carried a blazing mattress up the ladder and threw it over the side. Their fire-fighting was providential, as there was dripping fog oil all over the decks and wreckage.

When they started their engines they found they could go ahead, but only to port, even when backing down on the starboard engines, so they had to make a circle in towards the two blazing LSTs before heading away from them.They had ungripped their six lifeboats at the beginning of the action, so they immediately lowered the five undamaged boats and powered them up, to aid in heading the ship.

Some while later they received a signal to proceed to Brixham. They protested, believing there were no adequate medical facilities at Brixham, and were given leave to proceed to Dartmouth where they arrived early in the afternoon of the 28th. There were just four men killed during the action, eight missing and 18 wounded, one of whom died at the base hospital. All those were Navy men. Army casualties were four wounded. The commander of the LST 289 was both lucky and skilful that night, and many of his crew undoubtedly owed their lives to him. He later wrote:

> It will be observed that at no time were we given any apparent support from our escort or any other source, even though 33 minutes elapsed between the surface fire and the torpedo attack. It is to be hoped that future operations will avoid such futile sacrifices.

The comments of the commander of the LST 499 were in the same vein. The speed of advance of the convoy had been set too slow, he felt. Lack of information led them to believe that flares and gunfire were part of the exercise instead of enemy action. There was clearly an insufficient number of escorts. After the attack was made no orders or instructions were received and no rendezvous was given in case of scattering if attacked. In a nutshell, they had absolutely no idea what tactics to adopt if they came under attack, and they were almost without defence. Yet this was in waters which were regularly patrolled by German E-boats. The loss of life in this brief action – 197 sailors and 441 soldiers – was actually much greater than the invasion forces suffered on D-day itself at Utah Beach.

For their part, the Germans had a successful night. On their way southwards, back to base, the E-boats reported that they were involved in several actions with escorts – Günther Rabe thought with gunboats as well as destroyers. They managed however to return to Cherbourg without any losses. At that time and for many years afterwards, Rabe was of the opinion that they had hit an empty LST heading towards a port of embarkation for the expected invasion. The commander of the 9th Flotilla, Kapitan zur See Rudolf Peterson was awarded Oakleaves to his Knights Cross for the most successful killing of World War II, on 28 April 1944 in the English Channel. The 9th flotilla's total was: S-130, 1/2 Kill (shared with S-150), sunk LST 507; S-145, 1 Kill, sunk LST 531; S-150, 1/2 Kill (shared with S-130), sunk LST 507 and 1 Kill, damaged LST 289.

On the Allied side, it was time to count the cost. In fact, Tiger was observed by three of the most senior Allied commanders in the European theatre of war: Generals Dwight Eisenhower and Omar Bradley, and Air Chief Marshall Sir Arthur Tedder. Ike watched from a distance and left the scene of the exercise early, apparently disturbed by delays in the timetable. For those who were most closely involved, the first question was under whose authority the whole exercise had taken place, and about this there was little doubt. Normally, control of the waters of the English Channel was divided into three sections, and split among the commanders-in-chief at Plymouth, Portsmouth and the Nore, covering the western, central and eastern sectors respectively. The Slapton Assault Training Area fell within the sector commanded by Admiral Sir Ralph Leatham, who was based at Plymouth. Leatham had appreciated that problems might arise over the exercising of American forces from both the Army and Navy within his sphere of operations. The US naval forces concerned were designated the Eleventh Amphibious Force with Rear Admiral John L Hall in command. So shortly before Operation Duck, the first large-scale exercise to be held in the western Channel area, Leatham clarified his position to the American commander. His letter was dated 1 January 1944.

> I feel it is desirable to put on record my view of the relations in which you and I stand during the execution of the operation.
>
> Broadly speaking, I apply the customs and traditions of the British service, which I believe accord closely with yours, and I regard you in exactly the same light as any British flag officer in command of a British force operating within my command.
>
> It is my conception, therefore, that from the time of leaving Falmouth you are in tactical control of your forces, including the British vessels forming the close escort. Should I have any informatiorn of enemy attack by E-boat, submarine or air, it will be passed to you to take such action as you may think fit. I regard myself free to suggest action if necessary. I consider it is within your discretion to modify or cancel on account of weather or other causes. I myself retain full control of the covering forces throughout the operation unless or until otherwise ordered. You will of course be kept informed.
>
> I also retain an overriding control, should there arise circumstances which render it strategically necessary for me to cancel or curtail the exercise. I cannot at present see any likelihood of such circumstances arising.

The irony of the remarks about E-boat attack and the unlikely event of the exercise being curtailed would not have been lost on the American soldiers and sailors on board the LSTs that night. As it was, a full enquiry was demanded and the precise areas of responsibility of the various naval officers in the chain of command below Leatham were examined. American concern was voiced forcefully to Rear Admiral Leatham over the lack of escorts, in particular the absence of the destroyer, *Scimitar*, and the failure to provide a replacement. In his reply to Rear Admiral Hall, the British admiral apologised and offered his profound regrets. We shall return to the investigation, and the aftermath of the exercise from the point of view of the men who took part. But first, let us look more closely at what it was like for those on board the LSTs during the engagement and in the hours afterwards while they waited for rescue.

3

ATTACK!

'One lifeboat full of men capsized halfway down, spilling all of them into the water, and leaving the boat hanging uselessly.'

The official United States Navy records give precise times and bearings for the various manoeuvres of the convoy and for the moments each LST was hit, or sunk. But they also impart almost a sense of order to what was a night of virtual chaos from the point of view of the men actually aboard the LSTs. They lived or died knowing little and understanding less of what was going on around them, or what they should be doing. Over the years, my work on the tank has brought me into contact with a considerable number of veterans and I have collected more and more eye-witness accounts from survivors – some even written at the time, despite the wartime censorship. From their accounts, I have been able to put together a much more detailed picture of what it was really like the night the E-boats attacked.

One account I have is from Dale Rodman, who was a 20 year-old corporal in the 33rd Chemical Decontamination Company assigned to LST 507. He boarded the ship on the morning of 26 April, with 50 other men from the 33rd. The unit found that they were required to sleep at three separate locations around the ship. Each soldier was issued with an inflatable life belt containing two capsules of compressed carbon dioxide, which inflated the belt when punctured by squeezing it at a particular point. But no instructions were given to anyone as to how they should be used. And worse still, because the soldiers were in battle dress – with backpacks, rifles and suchlike - they found it more convenient to wear their belts round their waists instead of under their armpits. This would prove to be a fatal mistake for many.

The LST 515 – captained by Commander Skahill – led the convoy, followed by the LSTs 496, 511, 531, 58, 499, and 289, with the 507 last. Nobody on the 507 knew where they were heading or what the exercise was really all about, except the captain – Captain James Swarts – who had sealed orders which were not to be opened until they were well under way. When they left they could see two British corvettes in close attendance. But the warships later turned round and left the convoy, and the LSTs continued on their way, loaded down with Army personnel and equipment. There were the usual pastimes of card games, crap games, men writing letters, soldiers with guitars, singing and joking.

Shortly after boarding, Rodman was told that all corporals aboard were to be put on guard duty. He, along with all other corporals of the 33rd, was given duty on the first tour. They were told to check the bulletin board each day for future assignments. Rodman was assigned to a post on the tank deck from 12 midnight until 4 am on the 26th. The tank deck was loaded with amphibious trucks (DUKWs), conventional trucks and half-tracks. Indeed he recalled later they were jammed in so tight he could not walk between them. That first night passed uneventfully, except that Rodman learned to drink coffee which, unlike most of his countrymen, he had not much liked until then.

Several times during the days of the 26th and 27th the General Alarm was sounded, sending troops and sailors scrambling to their assigned positions around the ship. The 33rd was given an assembly point forward on the port side of the LST 507. Each time there was a drill, they were told what disembarkation procedures they were to follow and that if it were a real emergency they would be given further instructions over the loud speakers. But no one ever gave them any instructions about abandon ship procedures or what they should do in case of an attack.

Ironically, a story was going around that LST-type landing craft were so shallow-draughted that they could not be torpedoed by submarines. Nobody said anything about E-boats.

When Rodman checked the bulletin board on the 27th for

guard duty assignments, he saw the name E Redman had been assigned the 12 midnight to 4 am shift for the 28th on the tank deck. He saw no other names from the 33rd, but more than happy to avoid another tour of guard duty, he decided this 'Redman' was not meant to be him, and went to his bunk that night. He learned later that the officer of the day came to another of the sleeping areas of the 33rd looking for an E Redman and was told the 33rd had no such person. The officer assigned a Corporal Rosiek, also from the 33rd, to that shift. Corporal Rosiek did not survive. He was on the tank deck when the torpedo hit and exploded, causing petrol to ignite and ammunition to explode simultaneously. That typographical error saved Rodman's life.

At about 2 am on the 28th he was awakened by a loud noise which sounded like metal striking metal, followed shortly by the sounding of the General Alarm. He guessed the loud metallic bang was made by a glancing blow from a torpedo that did not detonate, and began waking those around him as several had not heard either the bang or the alarm. Rodman shouted to them to get on deck because a torpedo had just hit the ship and failed to explode. But the response from many was that they were not going on deck for just another dry run, and that anyway the ship could not possibly be torpedoed. Dale Rodman takes up his story in his own words:

> Four or five others and I from the 33rd went immediately to our assigned spot forward on deck. We had just arrived there when a terrific explosion threw everybody up in the air from the deck. I landed on my knees, losing my rifle. I saw flames coming from midships on the starboard side and people began scrambling about in all directions. Navy men were trying to use hoses to extinguish the fires, but there was no water pressure. Others were trying to lower the lifeboats manually because there was no electric power. A friend and I tried to help but were told to let the Navy do their job. Then we saw soldiers begin to jump into the water. I shouted that they should wait until the abandon

ship order was given before going over the side; the safest place to be was aboard ship as long as it was not going to sink. Finally, however, it became clear to all of us that it was time to abandon ship, even though we heard no such order.

My life jacket's carbon dioxide cartridges had been discharged in the confusion which meant the jacket would provide little or no support, so I looked for alternatives to jumping over the side. Immediately below, a lifeboat was still in the water alongside, and I was able to climb down the rope webbing that was hanging on the side of the LST. Climbing down, I saw that people already aboard the lifeboat were slipping into the water. Chaos reigned. When I got aboard I saw a sailor was hammering with a heavy object against the grappling hook which held the lifeboat to the 507. The LST was tilting to the right and the rear cable was too short and was holding the lifeboat out of the water. The sailor yelled out that he could not release the hook, and that we would have to abandon the lifeboat and take our chances in the water. I yelled to a soldier standing nearby to lend me his rifle to shoot the cable in two. The soldier did not even pause, but held his rifle next to the cable and fired. It parted after only one shot, and the lifeboat settled into the water. We could escape.

The Navy pilot accelerated the engine and we pulled away from the sinking ship. There were about fifteen people aboard the lifeboat when it pulled away, and from the light of the burning ship we could see another still along side the ship at the rear of the LST and a further one amidships, hanging part way down. We pulled away further from the sinking LST and began to pick up people from the water. I was startled to see scores of dead soldiers floating in the water with their packs and lifebelts on. The backpack and the lifebelt around their waists made them top heavy and they were lying on their backs with their heads under water. They had been knocked unconscious by the impact of hitting the water when they jumped overboard with their belts inflated, and they had drowned before they regained consciousness. Those of us on the lifeboat located what survivors we could in the darkness from the sound of their cries for help. Altogether there were between fifty and sixty survivors aboard when we were picked up by a British destroyer, HMS *Onslow*, at about 6:30 am. As I climbed to safety, I looked out over the water and saw hundreds of bodies still floating there.

Rodman tells the story very much from a soldier's point of view, unsure of what was happening, and bitter at not having been briefed on how to act in an emergency. For the Navy personnel on board the 507, however, things were not that much easier. Angelo Crapanzano was a first class petty officer on the LST 507. For him the most important event of the day they set out was that all the crew received tetanus booster shots. It was to be one of the reasons he survived.

On the second evening, Crapanzano started to feel feverish. His engine room watch was to be midnight to 4 am – the same timing as Dale Rodman – and he was to be in charge. But when he lay down in his bunk, he realised at once he had a fever because he could feel his pulse racing. Crapanzano was worried about his engine room watch coming up at midnight. When it came time to go he went down to the engine room with three other men feeling quite ill and wondering how long he could take it. Just then the engineering officer came down. Crapanzano told him he was not feeling well and was ordered to go up to sick bay. There, the pharmacist mate took his temperature, and found it was 104.

He told Crapanzano he had no business being out of his bunk. Crapanzano knew the fever was from the tetanus booster because he had had the same reaction in basic training camp. So, still feverish, he went back to the engine room and told the engineering officer what had happened in the sick bay. The officer replied that he should go up to his bunk, and that he would stand watch instead. By this time it was about 1 am.

Crapanzano returned to his bunk, and as he did so, he had a strange feeling, quite separate from the fever. It was as if somebody was telling him, 'find your life jacket and put it next to your bunk.' Life jackets were carelessly thrown all over crew quarters – half the time the men did not even wear them to their stations. He looked for his jacket , and found it on top of a locker – his inevitable nickname, 'Crappy', was written across the chest. He took it and laid it in the bunk next to his head. Almost at once, he fell asleep.

The next thing he knew, the action stations horns were blasting. Crapanzano jumped out of his bunk, put on the Mae West life jacket, ran to the ladder, and climbed down to the engine room. He looked at his watch; it read 1:55. 40mm guns were firing up above. He asked an officer what was going on. The man shook his head and said, 'I guess they're trying to make it as real as possible.'

Crapanzano's duty was to make all necessary changes of speeds on the engines as they were sent down from the wheelhouse on the annunciators, and to record them in the engine room logbook. The last thing he recorded was at 2:3. Suddenly there was a deafening roar, and everything went black. He felt himself lifted up and then came down and hit his head on something. He blacked out for a few seconds, then felt cold water coming in around his legs. He scrambled up the ladder. The torpedo had hit the auxiliary engine room in the heart of the ship. It was the next compartment forward of the main engine, where Crapanzano was stationed. The six men actually in the auxiliary engine room itself could never have known what happpened.

There was no power and no light. They could not fight the fire because the pumps would not run. When Crapanzano went topside, the scene was complete panic and confusion. Crapanzano recalls:

> The ship was burning furiously from the bow almost right down to the stern. Even the water was burning around the ship. There was fuel oil burning in the water because some of the storage tanks had ruptured from the force of the explosion. The Army DUKWs on the tank deck were loaded with petrol – all of those were burning too.
>
> Our skipper, Captain Swarts, ordered that we start to throw our ammunition over the side. So lines were formed and we started dumping the cans of 40 mm shells over the

side. This had lasted for about 10 minutes when the captain saw that there was no hope for us, so he gave the order to abandon ship. At that very moment, while we were standing on the stern of the ship, another torpedo just missed hitting us by no more than 10 feet. We watched the wake as it approached and passed. It was a terrifying moment.

We abandoned ship about 30 minutes after we got hit. The confusion and panic was unbelievable. The Army men they had aboard knew little about disasters at sea. I had my Mae West life jacket on, as did most of the Navy crew. The Army men had their carbon dioxide cartridge belts on, and it was obvious to us that they were wearing them wrongly – around their waists, instead of up under their armpits. But it was too late to tell them by then.

There were men jumping on top of men already in the sea. It was almost impossible not to hit somebody as more and more jumped into the water. After I jumped in, I swam towards the stern of the ship, about the only place where the water was not actually burning. A number of soldiers and Navy men were hanging on the tail section by the screws, which were already well out of the water. The ship was starting to list. Everybody had the same thought, 'What do we do now?' The water was ice-cold.

All at once, one of the ship's large oval life rafts came drifting towards us . It was smoking because it had floated through the burning water. The whole inside section was burnt away, but the outer ring had survived the flames and it was still buoyant. We all grabbed it, just managing to hang on with our arms wrapped around the ring. There were 11 of us. The first thing we had to do was to kick our legs, to get away from the ship and the burning water, which now almost completely surrounded the ship. We kicked furiously, and it helped keep us warm in the freezing water.

It was a weird feeling, not knowing where we were or how far we were from shore. It was pitch dark and we had no idea who had hit us or whether they were still around. We wondered if we would be picked up, and made prisoners. Or perhaps our own ships will come back to get

> us. Will they send help? We finally managed to get a fairly good distance from the LST, which was starting to show signs of going under.

There were men shouting, screaming, praying and dying, all around them. The cold water was starting to take its toll. The minutes passed into hours and still there was nothing but darkness. But the crying and yelling and screaming and praying had tapered off. The men were falling asleep, and letting go of the rafts – and dying. Three of the soldiers clinging to the raft said they were going to make a swim for it. Crapanzano tried to talk them out of it, telling them they had no way of knowing what direction they were going. But they went all the same.

An Army captain went completely berserk, and let go of the raft yelling and screaming madly.

When the LST 511 came back to pick up survivors at dawn, there were only two of them left on the raft out of the 11 that had started out. The soldiers were all gone. Crapanzano had been in the water for about four and a half hours. After three hours he could no longer feel his legs. From his waist down he was paralysed by the penetrating coldness of the water. He was very concerned about the possibility of his legs having to be amputated, but he remained convinced that the 104 degrees fever he had when he hit the water helped him fight the numbing cold. He also admits, with some candour, that one thing that kept going through his mind all night, while he hung onto the raft, was that he had never had a woman, and he could not leave the world in that condition.

When he saw a small lifeboat from the LST 511 approaching the raft, he gave up and passed out. He knew that he had made it. When he came to he was lying in a bunk on the LST 511. The first question he asked was 'How are my legs?' The medical orderly in charge said he saw no serious problems.

The story of the freeing of the jammed lifeboat, as told by Dale Rodman, is one which many survivors of the 507 recall. But there is only one first-hand account by the soldier who fired the rifle. He was Sergeant Stanley Stout. Sergeant Stout was in the First Amphibian Engineer Brigade. His unit was to clear a path through mine-fields inland so that both men and vehicles could move ahead rapidly and expand the beachhead. Stanley Stout's story stands out as one of the most crucial moments in the sinking of the LST 507.

Around midnight, most of his men had moved from the deck down into the hold to bed down and get some sleep, since they would make their run to the beachhead about 5 am the next morning. Stout had bedded down in the back of a DUKW with several members of his unit and soon it was very quiet.

After a short time he felt and heard a heavy dull thump in either the bottom or side of the ship. At first, he thought they had touched bottom and were docking on the beach. Then, about five minutes later another heavy dull thud was felt by Stout and several other men as well. This time, he got up and decided to go on deck to report it or find out the reason for the noise. He started for the stairs that led up to the forward deck and went to the door that opened to the outside. As he opened the door, he says:

> All hell broke loose – shell fire, machine gun fire – blue tracer shells were exploding on our forward deck. The din was terrific.
>
> The men in the hold were now running up the steps to get out on deck. I tried to keep them back at first. Then I finally let them out but ordered them to keep crawling to avoid being cut to pieces in the crossfire. Those out in the open were in total panic and many were falling to the deck hit by what seemed to be incoming fire. Just as I went on deck, a tremendous explosion shook the ship. It felt like an earthquake, with the deck literally jumping up and down. The oil lines, petrol tanks, fuel storage, ammunition and explosives all started to explode at once, burning and creating panic on the ship. Many men near me were jumping into the sea even though the flames were already burning in the water around the ship.
>
> I looked over the entire forward deck for any sign of officers or senior nco's but there were none in sight. I

checked the stairway to see if any more men were left downstairs. But by now the smoke was so thick that those of us on deck could not get anyone else out from below, and all the time more men in panic were jumping over the side into flaming water. In searching for someone on the ship who knew the lifeboat procedures or abandon ship procedures, the soldiers under my command could find no Navy officers or any of their own unit's Army officers. In fact, all five of our unit's officers had died at once, caught below deck when the torpedo struck and killed immediately.

I then saw a crowd forming on the rear deck, where efforts were being made to lower the lifeboats. The fires, smoke, and explosions were now growing and it was obvious that we had to abandon ship. But at no time had we heard any order to do so. The major fires seemed to be near the bridge or center of the ship. But explosions were getting more and more frequent and this was now our main concern.

I saw one lifeboat being lowered full of men, but halfway down it capsized, spilling all the men into the water and leaving the boat hanging uselessly in a vertical position. One boat was lowered safely, but the rest of those to the rear of the LST were all damaged and useless. The petrol tanks on the vehicles were now exploding almost continuously from the heat, and thick black smoke was billowing above the ship. The forward deck was getting so hot we could feel the heat through our boots. Some men were trying to release several of the large life rafts so they could get them over the side, but they gave up because they could not get them loose from the deck.

I made my way to the lifeboat that was left on the forward deck and helped as they started working to lower it into the sea. In spite of the heat and exploding ammunition, we were able to get it down into the water. Several Navy men then threw a net over the side so the soldiers could climb down into the boat, but many of the men now seemed so confused and in such a state of shock that they made no move. The sailors guided them to the net and they then climbed down into the boat. It was clear now that it was

> impossible to stay with the ship and any remaining men on deck were rapidly jumping into the sea.
>
> It was also obvious that the ship might soon blow completely apart (as later it did). But after filling the lifeboat with about 40 men we could not loosen the cables that ran from each end up to the davits. They were rusted solid and would not unhinge. The Navy men worked on them furiously, but to no avail. I told them to get the motor going on the boat while I went back onto the deck and looked to see what I could do to release the cables. I climbed back up the net to the deck and started working with my bare hands on the cables, but still they would not budge. Most of the men had now cleared the deck and gone overboard, but I recognised one member of my unit lying on deck with his face badly burnt and one trouser-leg burned off. He was unconscious and very bloody. I grabbed him by the shoulders, pulled him to the rail and pushed him over the side. Then I took his rifle and fired three shots into each cable. The cables split and fell away into the sea, releasing the lifeboat. I scrambled back down the net and into the boat and at last we pulled away from the LST.

For the next half hour or so, they stopped to pick up men, until they had close to 60 on board. Stout, as senior nco, continued to give orders to take on survivors until the Navy men warned him they were so overloaded that any additions might capsize them.

They pulled out about half to three quarters of a mile from the burning LSTs and hove to. They could hear the cries for help from all over the sea. This was the hardest part; to watch literally hundreds of men die and not be able to do anything to help them. It was a horrible experience. The cries gradually became weaker and those in the boat could plainly hear the last words of dying men, usually 'God', 'Mother', or 'Help'. As the night wore on, the cries gradually became quieter and quieter until the only sounds left were the few explosions still coming from the burning LSTs. All the men they could see in the water were now dead. The sea water temperature was no more than 45 degrees at that time of year.

About daylight, a large vessel approached them out of the morning mist and they could only hope it was not an enemy ship. It was British and they slowly pulled alongside and threw a net down the side. A number of sailors came down to help the injured up to the deck. They were given hot tea, warm blankets and Stout was treated by a British medic for a gunshot wound above the right knee, a wound he had not until that moment even noticed.

One thing that all the survivors relate is a sense almost of unreality in what was happening to them. Ralph Bartholomay was a naval gunner on the LST 507. He remembers going to sleep thinking that this was nothing more than a pre-invasion manoeuvre, a dry run and then being awoken by the klaxon sounding the action stations – alarm. He recalls:

> Getting dressed is vague in my memory, although I remember putting on clean dungarees with empty pockets and no socks. Time was short. Taking my life jacket and steel helmet were automatic. All our drills stressed that, and that is probably the only reason I am still here. My battle station was at the aft 40 mm gun on the port side, where I was a tracker. Because we had no time for eye adjustment from the light, my visibility was just about zero. There was a gunfire director in out tub (gun position) to relay orders from the gunnery officer. He was in contact with the bridge. Word passed along indicated attacking boats coming from the French side of the Channel. This radar sighting was not a blip, but a single white line, indicating great speed. At about the same time we heard that our escort, a British destroyer, was about 40 miles away. We were on our own.
>
> Our armament did provide a sense of security – what we lacked in size, we had in quantity. However, word was passed not to fire. Tracer shells would reveal our position and outline the ship, and there was the danger of hitting others among our own ships. Evidently, there was no provision for alignment of the flotilla in case of attack. The throbbing of the screws was reassuring until that stopped – intelligence sources had revealed the existence of sonic

> homing devices in German torpedoes, and the screws were stopped to eliminate that threat. In retrospect, it is now clear to me that we were a large stationary target, dead in the water, with orders not to fire. Then everything started happening very fast. One torpedo was sighted passing under us, and then another. Because we didn't draw much water and the torpedoes were running deep, we were being spared. I don't remember anyone shouting a warning of the one that hit us, but I do remember that when it hit there was a blinding flash, followed by a deluge of water and debris. I can still picture the ship and men illuminated by the flash, like a flash shot of a camera. As far as we were from the point of impact, the water and debris fell all over us.

The fire took hold quickly, and it became obvious that the fire-fighting equipment could not cope. Bartholomay and the rest of the crew got the order to abandon ship. But the lifeboats they were assigned to could not be launched.

> As I climbed down to the main deck, preparing to abandon ship, a seaman called for help to start a 'Handy Billy', a petrol-driven water pump. It had a two-stroke engine and was a bitch to start even in good conditions – then even if it was started, there was no hose. But the man was frantic to get below and help the men out of the auxiliary engine room – he said he had heard them screaming. There was smoke pouring out of the hatch and entry would have been impossible. The only other escape route for that engine room was a hatch on the main deck, and that was covered with burning vehicles.

Realising there was no hope of rescuing his comrades trapped below, Bartholomay abandoned ship.

> 'Remove your steel helmet, fold your arms firmly across your chest, check the area below, jump, and then swim away from the ship.' We had rehearsed this many times in training camp, but there were a few new wrinkles here. We

never jumped in 50 degree water that was covered in fuel oil, there were no attacking vessels involved and we were always sure to be rescued in a hurry as our 'ocean' was a 100 foot swimming pool. When I surfaced, I was spitting salt water laced with fuel oil. There was only a slight chop on the surface as I swam away from the ship and the oil was smoothing that down. Whenever I opened my eyes, the fuel oil would cause them to sting and I had trouble looking around. After swimming for a while, I felt that I had travelled far enough to be safe from the suction of the sinking ship, so I stopped and rested. There were about 400 men on the ship when we sailed but the scene around me was strangely quiet.

Snatches of survival techniques kept flashing by in my mind, but I still hadn't fully recovered from the shock of the explosion and my reactions were sluggish. I remembered hearing that if I removed some clothing I would float higher, but then I would lose body heat faster. You figure that one out! A sailor swam up without a life jacket and he was tiring fast, so we stayed together for a while. I don't know how long it was as time was being measured in a different way now. We didn't do much talking, there wasn't much to say and the water was starting to dull our senses. Some time later, the sailor said he saw a friend close by with some wreckage to hang on to and said he was going to swim over to him. I don't know what he saw, I couldn't see anything and I tried to talk him out of it, but he went anyway. I never saw him again.

Someone called out 'sharks', but that was the last thing on my mind; I thought the water was too cold for sharks anyway. A light breeze and the current were beginning to gather the wreckage in a tighter area. It was dark again and I had trouble seeing, but I could make out shapes close by, nothing of any size but a lot of them. I felt something brush by me, it felt coarse and all I could think of were sharks. It wasn't moving so I touched it and tried to identify it, it resembled all the other shapes. I suddenly realised that what I had felt was clothing and that all the shapes were bodies.

I spotted some wreckage with a few people hanging on,

> so I swam over. These were the first live persons I had seen in a while and it was encouraging. We were holding on to a small piece of wreckage that wasn't too stable and one fellow was trying to sit up on it. Every time he tried, the object turned over and would spill us all into the water. It seemed almost like a game. No one became angry, we were all too tired. This is when I started to say the Lord's Prayer over and over. I was beginning to get drowsy, a bad sign in cold water, and praying supplied some hope. I was starting to slip in and out of reality, with the unreal parts getting longer, when I heard the faint sound of a boat engine with someone calling out. Maybe some day I will hear a more welcome sound, but that night it sounded like the answer to a prayer. When the boat came close enough, I saw it was the LST 515 come back to pick us up. I mustered up what strength I had left and swam over. It was the longest ten yards I ever swam.

Naturally, there were medical teams on board all the LSTs. But when it came to caring for the injured during the action, what they could do was limited. Eugene Eckstam MD was one of the physicians on duty aboard the LST 507, and after the alarm sounded he hurried to the wardroom, which was the First Aid station for the ship. There were two tables, fastened to the deck, a bench along the outer bulkhead, and a metal locker against the forward bulkhead, which held all the medical supplies. That was all there was on board an LST when in transit – later they would serve as temporary floating hospitals, but that would need more medical supplies. When Eckstam reached the wardroom, he was told that there had been some shooting, but it was not clear where it came from. The favourite theory was that it was a gunner on the next ship shooting at shadows. As it was all quiet by this time, Eckstam decided to go topside to see what was going on. That was when the torpedo struck.

> As I was passing the captain's door – BOOM!!! – followed rapidly by the sound of crunching metal, a painful landing on both of my knees on the steel deck,

falling dust and rust – then darkness and silence – and aching knees, and wondering, 'My God, what happened?'

There was no electricity, but I had done my homework and knew where every battle lantern was located. One was by my right hand as I stood up, just across the passageway from the captain's door. With this first light, the rest were easily found and used. The force of the explosion had popped the first aid cabinet partly off the wall and it was leaning out about 30 degrees with its doors open and supplies all over the wardroom. Casualties came in slowly, some by themselves and some by litter, but most were half carried. There were only a few. One fellow sustained a broken thigh and we fixed him up with a splint. As more reports of the damage came in, we realised that the mid part of the ship was an inferno and no one could pass from one end of the ship to the other, either on the main deck or below. So I decided to check out all the aft part of the ship that I could, to be sure there were no casualties needing care and to secure the ship. Secure means to close all the hatches between compartments to preserve buoyancy and delay or prevent sinking. Since the officers were otherwise busy, and since I knew what to do, I did it. . .

One of the most difficult decisions I have ever made, and one that gave me nightmares for years – and still does – was to close the hatches leading to the tank deck. I had tried to call and go through into the tank deck. But it was like looking into and trying to walk through a huge roaring furnace fire. Worst of all were the agonising screams for help from the Army men trapped in there. I can still hear them. But knowing there was absolutely no way anyone could help them, and knowing that smoke inhalation would end their miseries soon, I closed the hatches. Hatches can be opened or closed from either side.

After checking all the compartments possible, I returned to the wardroom. One or two other injured had been cared for. One of the officers came by and said the captain had given the order to abandon ship. This order really wasn't necessary because the fire was heating up all the metal and our feet were getting hot even through the thick soles of our combat boots.

Eckstam was reluctant simply to jump into the water. As a medical man he knew the effect of sudden cold water immersion on the human system. But none of the lifeboats in his section of the ship could be moved without electrical power. He checked out the smaller life rafts, but like so many others of his comrades he quickly discovered that their restraining pins were all rusted firmly into place. In the event, he scrambled down the cargo net which had been lowered to allow the men to escape, and swam away from the ship as quickly as possible to avoid the suction when it went down. He made it to a life raft and was picked up with a number of other survivors the following morning.

Further forward in the convoy, Clifford Graves MD was on board the LST 511. He went to bed about midnight, and was awoken by the alarm at just after 2 am. Thinking it was just a practice, he and the other medical officers were hesitant to get dressed, but their doubts were firmly put aside when one of the crew came running through, closing all the water-tight hatches, and shouted, 'This is it, boys. Ship torpedoed behind us.' They ran up on deck and saw the flames of what was the LST 507 burning brightly. Graves says:

> There was only one LST behind us now (it would have been the 531), and we could make out its outlines readily in the light of the moon. Suddenly there was a terrific explosion. It had a dull sound, as though a great heavy mass had fallen onto a heavily carpeted floor. The LST right behind us burst into a great mass of flames all at once. She seemed to have disintegrated with that one burst. Things began to happen on our own ship. It wasn't more than a minute and all hell seemed to break loose all around us. Coloured flashes of light. For a stunned second I didn't realise what they were. But then I knew. Tracer bullets. The yellow and purple ones were coming out of the water from the German E-boats. The pink ones were going into the water from our own anti-aircraft guns.
>
> There was a lot of shouting and confusion on deck. If I knew then what I have learned since, I would have fallen flat on my stomach and stayed there, but I didn't. I ducked my head and ran, and after what seemed an age finally

reached the middle portion of the ship, found a doorway and dashed in. I decided I'd better get to the wardroom, but as I came down the narrow corridor towards the wardroom, a soldier came running towards me holding his hands over his belly. 'I've been hit,' he cried. He fell down at my feet. I looked at his clothing and it appeared to be undamaged. I thought at first that maybe he was hysterical, but then I opened his shirt. There was a deep abdominal wound where a shell fragment or a splinter of metal had gone in. I had some soldiers carry him into the wardroom and soon other casualties began to be brought in. We administered first aid and treated shock; there was nothing else we could do at the time.

While we worked, the shooting on our boat stopped. It hadn't lasted very long – maybe a few minutes. But the show wasn't over. The E-boats sent a torpedo into the LST directly in front of us. Then some more shooting. The convoy was now broken up, it was every ship for itself. We headed for the nearest land, which was 20 miles away; we couldn't radio for help because there was radio silence, and to have used our radio would have meant giving away our position as well as that of the other boats which still remained afloat. I found out later that the captain of our ship had no chart, and no idea of the minefields that had been laid down by the British. Even if he had been able to call for help, it could never have got to us in time. The corvette that was supposed to be our protection, we never saw.

We sat and waited for the torpedo we knew would come. Our work was done. There was nothing to do but wait. But the torpedo never came. The only way we could figure it was that they had run out of torpedoes. Nothing else was there to stop them. At about six o'clock in the morning, in the grey mist, we were able to make out land. An hour later we were at anchor in the little harbour of Weymouth. Columbus himself couldn't have been happier at the sight of land than we were that morning.

4

A SLOW, COLD DEATH

'I looked out over the water, and saw hundreds of bodies still floating there.'

Most of the survivors have similar tales to tell of the confusion surrounding the E-boat attack and of the escape, or sinking, of their LSTs. Many of them, like Dr Eugene Eckstam, spent a long time in the water but remember little of it. The attack is vivid in their memories, but the hours of waiting in the numbing cold were either spent in a semi-coma, or perhaps memory has mercifully erased them. But among the scores of letters I have received from survivors of Exercise Tiger, one contains considerable detail of those hours of waiting for rescue.

Arthur Victor was a hospital apprentice, second class, on the LST 507. Quite against orders, he kept a diary of the events of the 'Night of the Bloody Tiger'. Against orders it may have been, but it provides the most moving account of the hours after the 507 went down.

Victor, like the others, was awakened by loud banging noises that sounded to him like hammers being pounded on the top deck. He had been sound asleep in an upper berth in one of the compartments with seven other sailors. He could hear other men scrambling around and shouting. He called out, 'What the hell's going on?' Someone shouted back from the darkness, 'We're under attack!'

He jumped from his bunk onto the cold deck and wasted no time getting dressed. But in the excitement and rush, he forgot his life belt, an almost fatal error.

He dashed from the compartment with the other men, pushing and shoving up the ladder to the topside. But when he went through the hatch and stepped on deck he was surprised to see how calm and quiet it was. No shooting, no shelling. In fact, it was – as he remembers it – 'a panorama of beautiful sky, lit up by a bright moon and a myriad of stars. The air was brisk and chilled and felt good. It did not seem a night for war.' Victor went to his battle station at the stern. The other men on duty were already there – Dailey, Lewis and Rutherford. They were all quietly staring out to sea.

He crouched at his post whispering to his colleagues about the incident and was told that the pounding he thought he had heard was actually tracer aimed at the gun turrets. Victor assumed they had been fired at from a submarine, or German E-boat. But because everything had gone so quiet, he also hoped that whoever it was had withdrawn and returned to base.

After a few minutes of silently waiting and staring out to sea, looking for any movement and seeing or hearing nothing, he walked to the railing on the port side and stood beside the raft. He was leaning on the rail, caught up in the beauty of the night, when he was joined by Rutherford who leaned against the other side of the raft. Feeling far from home, they started talking about girls they had known. Then, suddenly, there was a tremendous explosion.

Victor was lifted off his feet and hurled back against the bulkhead, his head smashed sideways against the steel plate so hard that he almost passed out. But fortunately his helmet absorbed the shock and he was merely dazed. Somehow, he hauled himself up and staggered back to the raft. Rutherford was at his side, his face ashen. Victor asked if he was OK. He said he was. Then he said Victor's mouth was bleeding. But as Victor ran his hand across his sleeve, he could only feel the ringing in his ears.

They looked down to the area where the blast had come from and saw flames and black smoke billowing from a gaping hole just about amidships. They realised at once that the torpedo had torn through the starboard side and exploded into the tank deck and engine room – a fatal blow. Although they knew the ship would go down, they were more immediately afraid of another attack which they might not survive. It never came.

But it was instant pandemonium. Men were already running around waving their arms and screaming hysterically 'We're all gonna die.' Some even ran past towards the inferno, then raced back screaming even more hysterically. Victor and Rutherford tried to grab hold of them to calm them down, but most just pulled away and ran off.

Then someone yelled, 'Men overboard!' They turned from the fire and saw some men already in the water, swimming around. All they could do was toss them life preservers. Some never made it. The men on deck saw them struggle and go under.

The gunnery officer was trying desperately to restore some order out of the chaos. He ordered the fire-fighters to set up their equipment then head to the fire. They fought the flames as bravely as they could, but the heat and smoke were so intense that the effort had to be abandoned. They fell back exhausted, gasping for breath. The fire raged on.

Meanwhile, some had crawled up the girder that held up the lifeboat hanging over them, and physically tried to pull it down. But the explosion had jammed the supports against the boat and it would not budge. In desperation they even tried to chop through the steel cables that held it with fire axes, flailing away with all their might, but never made a dent. Finally, they fell to the deck exhausted and screaming to the heavens in frustration. The boat was unmovable. It could have saved most of them. It would go down with the ship.

The stern was by this time packed with men who had been topside or came topside soon before or just after the blast. It was bedlam.

At this point the gunnery officer, Ensign Brown, ordered all the ammunition to be tossed overboard. The deck was getting very hot and they could have blown themselves up. As he saw the cartridges hit the water and sink from view Victor knew their situation was desperate.

Brown then ordered them to release the life raft. They removed the holding pins and gave it a shove. Over it went, but to their dismay it landed upside down, with the survival equipment underneath. So Brown asked for a volunteer to go over the side and keep it in tow. A sailor by the name of Star said he would go, and leaped overboard. Rutherford and Victor wanted to go too, but Brown said one was enough, so they stayed at their post and watched Star scramble onto the safety of the raft. That was where they wanted to be.

Now Brown shouted, 'Abandon ship', and men started over the side in droves. Many landed on top of one another. Those who survived the jump swam towards the raft. Arthur Victor takes up the story in his own words:

> I threw down my helmet and started over when I heard someone frantically calling for help. I turned and saw another corpsman standing there shaking with fear. He threw his arms around me and begged me not to leave. He was crying hysterically – moaning that he couldn't swim and was terrified of water. I said I wouldn't leave him as long as he did what I told him to do. Thank God he was wearing his life belt, which was inflated, so I took his hand, led him to the railing and told him we would jump together, but for God's sake don't grab onto me, instead of relying on his life belt for support. I had to keep reassuring him that we would be OK. Then we slowly climbed over the railing together and, before he had time to hesitate, I grabbed his hand and jumped, pulling him down.
>
> We hit the water together, our grasp broken as we sank deep into the freezing cold sea. It seemed an eternity before we reached the surface. I was immediately grabbed around the neck in a strangle hold, dragging me back under. He was so crazed with fear that he tried to kneel on my shoulders. I managed to fight him off and struggle to the surface, but he kept lunging at me with the ferocity of an animal and pushed me down so he could use my body to stand on. Again I was able to fight him off, kicking up and beyond him while gasping for breath. He came at me again, but this time I was ready. Holding him at arms length, I hit him repeatedly as hard as it was possible in the water, all the time screaming that he was drowning both of us. Finally he stopped and slumped in his belt, sobbing that we were all going to die. I told him that was bullshit and to stay calm and we would make it. Then I told him I would manoeuvre

us to the rail at the stern of the LST. Cautiously reaching out, I took hold of his belt. For once, the corpsman did not make a move. So I worked the two of us over to the rail where he climbed on and clung to it monkey-like for dear life. I stayed where I was, holding on and treading water, getting myself and my breath back in working order.

After a few minutes, I tried talking him down and heading for the raft, which to our surprise was still in sight, lit up by the burning 507. He refused to let go and just held on tighter to the rail, sitting on his haunches. I pulled on his legs and even tried to pry his hands loose, but he held on desperately. I threatened to go, and started to move away, but he begged and pleaded with me to stay. The 507 was sinking slowly at the stern now and I knew there was not much time left. Still he would not budge, and without a life belt I was far from sure I could make it to the raft myself if I delayed any longer. So I made one last effort to get him off, but still to no avail. I turned and started to move away. The man immediately screamed at me to come back. I stopped, turned and told him to let go and work his way over – it was no more than a few feet. But he said he was too scared and could not do it. Reluctantly I turned, wished him luck and swam away. I never looked back, even though he kept shrieking at me to return, calling out that he was sure he was going to die. I was sick at heart.

When I reached the raft, I was surprised to find that there was only a handful of men, clinging to the side. I had thought by now it would be overcrowded, but many who had survived the flames and the explosions had nontheless floundered and died before they could even get near. Star – who had originally jumped down and righted the raft – was kneeling on top. I found an open space on the side and took hold. It was not long before we were joined by others who swarmed alongside and quickly filled the remaining open spaces along the flanks of the raft. Those who did not make it to an open space had to hold onto those who did. It was made clear that only one man was to be allowed on top. This was not challenged – at first.

But the extreme cold and hysteria were already taking

their toll. Men without life belts and in waterlogged clothing were in a constant struggle to stay afloat, holding onto others with belts or Mae Wests. Even those with preservers were struggling because of the freezing water and the desperate state of panic most of us were in. Men were dying all around in those first few minutes. It puzzled me then how young, healthy men could give up and die so easily. It still does today. But as many as died, there were still as many to take their place, so the raft was quickly – and dangerously – loading up.

Then we spotted another raft about 200 yards away, but further out to sea, with just a cluster of men clinging to it. I volunteered to swim over and help relieve the load on their raft. Some of the others said they would go with me. So I removed my lifejacket, which had become heavy with water and would be a burden to swim in, and let it drift away. But in that short time the other raft had filled up, so I had to stay where I was. But now, without my life jacket, I was left bare from the waist up which put me at the mercy of the freezing cold water. It was like being washed in a pool of ice water.

We were no more than about 100 yards out from the LST when I felt a sharp burst of heat strike the back of my neck. Then someone started screaming hysterically that the water was on fire. I turned quickly and stared at flames and billowing black smoke making a wide circle around us. I did not think we were going to make it. I felt sure that the fire would overtake the raft or exhaustion would overtake me. I had to leave the raft; there was no other choice.

I was just about to push off, believing this would be the end for all of us, when by some miracle the fire suddenly died out not more than 20 feet away. It was, I thought, as though the hand of God reached down and turned off the flames.

I was shocked into disbelief, then I started shaking and sobbing quietly to myself with relief. I held onto the raft for dear life, emotionally drained, and thanking God for saving me as I rested and pulled myself together. Then I vowed that no matter what happened from then on I was not going

LSTs at Blackpool Sands, a neighbouring beach to Slapton Sands, before the disaster.

Troops and vehicles, including LCVP 201, a halftrack and a Sherman tank with flotation 'skirts' at Slapton Sands.

LCTs 149 and 495 at Slapton Sands.

Troops off-loading from LCVP from LSTs 624 and 85 at Slapton Sands. LCI 85 was lost during the Normandy operation in June 1944.

View from an LCT showing the rolling Devon countryside with the troops looking relaxed. I assume the picture was taken before the disaster.

This image of the D-Day rehearsals could well have come from The Longest Day.

Talking to the locals. I have not been able to identify the people involved.

Supplies and preparations for the exercise.

Damage on shore caused by the bombardment.

Aftermath – LST 289 limps into Dartmouth Harbour after being torpedoed.

to become that terrified again. I had seen how hysteria had caused so many to die needlessly, and I was not going to let that happen to me. I reasoned that if I kept patient and calm and took things as they came I knew I could make it.

There were about 75 of us now, jammed around and about the raft, holding onto it and each other as before. Men came and men went. It was hard to keep count.

Across from me were six other corpsmen clinging to the side, including my buddy Rutherford, who had one of them hanging on piggy back. One of the doctors was to the left of him at one end, holding up a soldier who kept moaning that his leg was broken. The other doctor was opposite. My friend Dailey was not there. Neither was Lewis. Next to me was a black mess steward, huddled in his jacket with the collar wrapped around his face. He looked as though he was trying to hide.

We were so packed in that the raft was an arm's length under water from the sheer weight of it. It was shaped like a postage stamp and did not feel that much bigger. So we had to extend our arms to keep our heads above water. It was agonising.

Men were dying off all around. Those without life preservers just let go, struggled a bit, then disappeared. Dead weight made it impossible to do anything to help them. The men they were holding onto tried their best, but the freezing water was still taking its toll, preservers or no preservers. One of the first to go was a corpsman who was only 19 years old, married and the father of a four-month-old son. He was not wearing a life belt and had been holding on next to Rutherford. Suddenly, and without warning, he was struggling in the water, screaming for help. Star could not reach him and Rutherford, who was still holding up the other sailor, threw him his leg to grab on to. He managed to get hold of the foot, but slid off and sank beneath the surface. We waited what seemed an age for him to come up, but he never did. In a twinkling he was gone. We were dumbfounded and devastated and prayed for him. It was all we could do.

But no sooner was he gone than the boy on Rutherford's

> back let go and started sliding down too. Rutherford reached back to try and hold him up, but he was too heavy and wet and kept going straight down. Star tried to help, but it was too late. He never said a word, and never tried to stop himself. He just quietly disappeared beneath the surface and never came up. He was the second one of them to go. It happened to be his 19th birthday. We could only pray for him too.

They could see the 507, still afloat, and still aflame, listing at the stern. There were men still running about her decks. Off to the left was the LST 531 and they started kicking in her direction, hoping to be picked up. Then they heard two thunderous explosions and saw great columns of fire and smoke rising from the belly of the ship. Ammunition started firing from the bow guns and shot straight up into the sky. It looked to them almost like a Fourth of July celebration, except for the macabre addition that bodies were being hurled from the deck like so many rag dolls – bodies and parts of bodies too. A few men managed to jump and swim for their lives as the 531 split and went down. But in a matter of minutes, as if in the blinking of an eye, it blew up and disappeared, taking most of its crew and soldiers with it. It was a nightmarish sight.

When the 531 went down, many of those on the raft with Victor started shrieking despairingly that it was the end of the world. They cried that they would be gunned down in the water. Desperate men were praying aloud, begging and pleading to be saved. They started packing in closer and tighter to the raft, pushing it further under. The situation started to get very tense.

> Then a few soldiers banded together, and worked their way closer, threatening to get on the raft and take it over. They said that because we were sailors, we were fish-like and better in the water than the army men. They complained they did not have life belts and should be allowed on the raft. I showed them that I had no life belt either and they

could see that I was half naked. They argued I was a sailor and could swim and was used to this sort of thing. I assured them that getting torpedoed was not a daily occurrence for me and the ability to swim was not a Navy requirement. Star whispered that he was afraid they would pull him off. So to stop a bad situation getting even worse I finally told them that anyone who tried to mount the raft, would be pulled off or pushed under. We would do whatever it took to keep them off, and keep the raft from being swamped. My heart was pumping as I really expected to be in a dogfight. But to my relief the leader never made a move and the others backed off too. They grumbled, but they never made a concerted charge, and it ended up in no more than a staring match.

We drifted quietly on. I had almost become unbearably cold by now. I had also been swallowing oily tasting salt water, which had made me nauseous, and I started puking. I urinated in my trousers to feel the warmth - it felt good pouring over my thighs. But I still kept vomiting violently. Meanwhile, the black mess steward who was on my right during all this time had been trying to keep a low profile. He had snuggled up to me and held on tightly. Up to this point he was all right. But suddenly someone shouted, 'Get that nigger off there.'

I felt him stiffen and move even closer. I put my arm around the man and shouted back that he had as much right as anyone to be there and anyone who tried to pull him off would have to deal with me personally. I felt sorry for the little steward and saw no reason why he should be left to drown simply because he was black. I told him to stay close and not to worry. We waited for an answer or for someone to make a move, but no one did. The mess steward never said a word and never left my side.

Across from me on the raft, at the corner to my left, was Scott, one of my three close buddies who had been having a hard time hanging on. From the start he was in a state of panic and kept begging and pleading to get on the raft, asking me over and over again to help him. Star and I kept up a steady chatter to try and calm him down, but it did no good. He did not seem to hear. He kept pleading and even tried to get on, but we had to keep him off. I kept yelling at him to hold on, then realised that I would have to leave my spot and go to his side, as difficult as that would be. I had just told Star what I planned to do when someone called over that he thought Scott was dead. I looked over and saw that the man was no longer moving. He was bobbing in his belt, head down, with his hands at his sides. Star checked him for any sign of life, but got no response. Star told me he thought Scott was dead too, certainly he was not breathing. I told Star to feel his neck for a pulse – there was none. Then I told him to place Scott's head under water and look for bubbles. He did, but none came. We had seen enough dead already not to believe he was dead too. I told Star there was no choice but to let him go and leave his belt on, which is what we did. Someone else moved into his spot.

With heavy hearts we saw him drift away. I wanted to rage when I saw him go. It was such a waste. Then I wondered, and I still wonder, was he really dead? How could he be, when he was so vibrant and full of life? How could he die like that? The doubt would live in me all the rest of my days.

Victor was numb as they continued drifting and losing men. They seemed just to give up and slip under without much of a struggle, or died in their life preservers where they were. He just could not understand how men so young could die so easily. He thought it must be from shock or heart failure, or fear, never thinking it could be from the extreme cold. After all, he was unprotected and as cold as the rest, and had lost all feeling in his legs. Still he never dreamed he could die because of it. As miserable as he was, he just thought, 'To hell with it! Stay cool and not cold and you'll be OK.'

The LST 507 was still in sight, but fast fading from time. Fog was beginning to surround them; they could still hear cries for help. They called out and flashed their light to give their position, but only a few managed to swim over to them. Rutherford had stomach cramps by this time and was doubled over on the edge of the raft in great pain. He was no longer sure he could make it. Another corpsman, directly across, asked Victor to take his hand, and hold him up so he could lay his head down. They held hands, off and on, for most of the night.

They finally drifted out of sight of the burning 507, shrouded in mist and fog. They heard the drone of an engine, hoping it wasn't the Germans looking for survivors to pick off. But someone said it sounded like one of their small boats, so they took the chance and yelled and shouted and kept signalling with a flashlight that they were able to pull free from the underside of the raft. But the boat never came. Later they learned it was only picking up lone swimmers.

They continued drifting in a thick fog and heavy swell. Men became seasick and threw up – taking in water as they gulped, which made them sicker and weaker and more hopeless. The cold water splashed over them as they bobbed up and down, up and down, up and down. They were a pitiful bunch, to say the least.

> Guys were now dying off in a steady stream. They died and drifted away, or died and went under, or just died where they were. The man holding onto me from behind died in his Mae West. I had to stare into the lifeless eyes of someone so close, yet unknown to me. We tried to remove his jacket, but it was impossible to untie it, so we had to push him away and let him drift off into the darkness. Someone else took his place and grabbed hold of my belt. No one spoke very much.

With the loss of so many men, the raft had been slowly rising to the surface, so they could at last lean on it. The soldier with the broken leg was allowed on top, where he sprawled out. He was a big man and covered almost the entire top of the raft. But with him on top and the rest leaning, the raft went under again, and so they were back to extended arms and hands held high. It was as if they were back to square one, and Victor wanted so very much to plant his feet and feel solid ground beneath him. It was maddening just to dangle and feel nothing but a bottomless pit under him. He yearned for a bit of relief, to be on top of that raft for just a little time, but it was never to be.

At some point in the night they were joined by Lewis, a bear of a boy, who just came swimming out of the darkness. Victor could not believe it. He acted as if it was all nothing unusual. When they asked where he came from he just said, 'Out there, where the other raft and boat were drifting around.' He had given up his spot at the raft, and being an excellent swimmer swam around, keeping the boats and rafts within earshot. He said he could hear the others, so he was not afraid. Victor wanted him to stay but he said no, and after resting a few minutes he said goodbye and swam away. Amazingly enough, he survived. He was picked up later, all alone, swimming around. To Victor, he was a hero.

Around dawn, after about five hours in the water, they were down to about 20 men left alive. The raft had risen to the surface once more and they were able to lean again. It felt wonderful. But it was still dark and the fog had not lifted. Victor was quite numb and exhausted. He wanted to put his head down and sleep. Even though they were at the surface, Victor was still holding the other boy's hands across the raft. That was what he wanted and it helped to keep him settled down. But it was tiring. The little black mess steward was still hanging on too, and seemed none the worse for wear. He still had not said a word.

As the hours drifted by, Victor thought of home, family and friends. He even thought of dying and considered the alternative ways to go. He was no longer afraid. He just faced the reality of the situation and if he had to die, well so be it, but without pain. The thought of drowning did not appeal. Laying his head down and going to sleep was an option. Then he thought, 'What the hell am I doing? I'm not going to die.' He thought of how pointless it would be to die like this, so he picked himself up, dusted himself off, and forgot about the idea. He knew if there was to be one left it would be he. He would not give up on the others, and would not give up on himself either. It was a good feeling.

> Daylight was starting to break, but not fully, when someone started yelling that he could see a ship. We all thought he had gone mad, when suddenly we saw the outline of a warship loom before us as though it had risen out of the water. We did not know if it was enemy or friendly, and did not much care. We started shouting and drifted close enough to see a small boat being lowered from an LST. It hit the water and headed in our direction. We would be saved!
>
> The boy whose hand I had been holding said he was OK. So I released my grip. Certainly, the boy seemed all right. The lifeboat pulled up to the raft, at the short end to my right, with the bow door down. But it started taking in water, so we were told to stay put as it had to back off. When it did, the boy leaped for a dangling rope, was dragged back, slid off and disappeared. With all the confusion he was gone in a moment. There was nothing we could do about it.

When the boat came back with its bow a bit higher, they scrambled off the raft in turn. But when Victor started crawling onto the bow the boat drifted back and he fell in between raft and boat, held up by his arms. The end of the bow door kept ramming his legs against the raft, but he felt nothing. Finally, someone grabbed him by the belt and hauled him into the boat and gave him a jacket. It felt like fur against Victor's skin. They were told to lie down and were covered with tarpaulin. They could never have stood anyway.

They were taken to the rescue ship, the LST 515. Some were hoisted on stretchers, others went up the ladder. Victor declined the stretcher and hauled himself and his dead legs up the ladder. It was his way of thanking God.

When they were all on board, they were led to the crews' quarters, stripped, given a shot of brandy, and put to bed. The men from the other raft were already there and greeted them as if it was party time. The corpsman Victor had left at the rail was among them. He would not speak to Victor. Later Victor learned that the man was coaxed and cajoled into working his way onto a raft, or know he would be left to die. As the raft was only a few feet away, by going around the stern he could jump rather than swim, so he did it. Despite his personal feelings, Victor was glad to see that the man had made it.

They slept for a while, got up, and watched the sailors haul dead bodies from the water. Corpses were strewn everywhere. For Arthur Victor, it was the most wretched sight of the war.

5

A QUESTION OF BLAME

'Did you make any protest on taking this convoy with only one escort?'

On 13 January 1986, I received a letter from the historical section of the Ministry of Defence. The Ministry conceded that E-boats were known to be active in the English Channel at the time of Exercise Tiger and patrols were disposed accordingly, to give warning and to intercept. It was the last step along a long road of investigation. Forty years after the event, the Ministry was finally prepared to admit that a large portion of the blame for what went wrong lay on the British side.

The letter said that the last ditch defence of the nine Landing Ships (Tank) in T-4 was intended to consist of the corvette HMS *Azalea* and the old destroyer HMS *Scimitar*, but, unfortunately, the latter was rammed and damaged by an American landing craft (Infantry) during the previous night's exercise and the dockyard at Plymouth was unable to take her in hand before 28 April. It was decided, without reference to the Staff (as the Ministry put it later), that she should remain in harbour although she was seaworthy in the calm conditions prevailing. Not until 11 pm on 27 April was the situation appreciated at the Plymouth naval headquarters, where the short-handed staff were severely stretched by the imposition of the invasion rehearsal arrangements on top of the normal conduct of their day to day operations. By the same token, the Plymouth Communications Organisation was similarly overloaded.

By the time that the senior officer, Escorts, in Start Bay was alerted to the fact that T-4 had only one escort, E-boats had already been reported by shore radar stations and by the destroyer HMS *Onslow*, which – according to the letter – engaged and drove off two of the craft. HMS *Saladin* left her patrol in Start Bay at 1:37 am on 28 April and proceeded at 23 knots towards the LST convoy, her speed limited by an unreliable boiler. Meanwhile, the *Azalea* was receiving the broad cross of enemy activity, but held to her ordered track: her instructions stated that she was to close the coast 'in the event of attack' not to forestall attack – the US Navy commander, Force U, Admiral Moon, was the operational commander and could have overriden the order but did not do so, although he too was in receipt of the warning signals.

The British information was that the E-boats, of the 5th and 9th Schnell-boote Flotillas, had left Cherbourg at 10 pm on 27 April and delivered their attacks between 2:10 and 2:15 am on 28th, the convoy being at that time about 15 miles to the westward of Portland Bill. The first that the *Azalea* knew of the attack was firing by one of the LSTs at 2:10 am and then hits on three LSTs at 2:15 am followed by further firing by the LSTs themselves. The E-boats were detected by the *Azalea*'s radar only after the attack and then only briefly; although they encountered a destroyer patrol during their withdrawal, they all returned to base safely.

The *Saladin*, which had expected to meet the convoy at 2:45 am, saw the tracers and the flash of the first hit on the LSTs. When she arrived on the scene she found a few boats from the LSTs picking up survivors and she herself rescued 129 men before hauling off to screen LST 515 which had by that time returned to assist in the rescue operations. The *Azalea*, which had shepherded the six undamaged LSTs towards the coast, returned to the area and escorted the damaged LST 289 to Dartmouth.

Such was the bald statement of the British involvement. But how could so many mistakes have been made? Surely it should have come as no surprise to anyone to find E-boats in that part of the Channel at that time. How could communications have broken down so tragically? Most of the British ships involved in the action have since been sold or broken up, or both. Few if any of their logbooks survive. However, a friend of mine has obtained a number of documents from British sources, which – together with what I have found from the Pentagon – allow us to put together a much more complete picture of what went wrong, and why, than has previously been known.

To begin with, an excerpt from the secret Plymouth Command War Diary of Events for the period 00:01 – 24:00 28 April 1944 reveals that at 00:11, HMS *Onslow*, patrolling off Portland Bill, encountered an E-boat on a northerly course which retired to the southward a few minutes later. At about 00:20 three further groups of E-boats were plotted between 10 and 20 miles west southwest of Portland Bill, steering northwest, and apparently searching to the northwestward. These groups were also plotted at Portland, but owing to ignorance of the disposition of forces dispersing from Exercise Tiger, the Portland plot was rather confused. No mention is made in the diary of the E-boats being engaged by the British forces.

Two hours later the two groups of E-boats attacked the Tiger convoy.

On retiring to the southward the enemy was sighted and engaged by HMS *Offa* and HMS *Orwell* (clearly the unnamed destroyers mentioned by Günther Rabe) but managed to escape at high speed under cover of smoke.

As for the *Saladin*, which was supposed to rendezvous with convoy T-4, her log does not survive either. But there is a report made by her commanding officer to Admiral Moon the following day, 29 April. In it, Lieutenant Commander P King, RN, notes that whilst on patrol in Start Bay to Mewstone under the orders of HMS *Tantaside*, he received the E-boat reports from HMS *Onslow* on broadcast channel 'CN'. On his going up to the bridge a signal was in the course of being made from *Tantaside* detaching him to join *Azalea* with convey T-4 in place of *Scimitar*.

This excerpt from a despatch by the Task Force commander confirms the late instruction:

> X HMS *Scimitar's* suffering slight damage although still operational resulted in a mixup in Plymouth command in

> regard to her orders and she was not sailed with convoy leaving corvette HMS *Azalea* as only escort X This was unknown to anyone in authority until discovered by Plymouth command too late to provide an additional escort before attack X *Saladin* proceeding to reinforce as result of CinC Plymouth action after discovery arrived in time to pick up survivors but not assist in repelling attack X Timely reports of E-boat movements from radar plot were made by CinC Plymouth X

Owing to the delay in receiving shore plots on the CN broadcast, the *Saladin* had little hope of intercepting individual E-boats except by chance; furthermore, her primary duty was to find and protect the remaining ships of the convoy. As it was, some time had been lost in searching for the convoy, which had not been reported as scattered, and in altering course towards the various bursts of tracer and starshell that had been seen. But even with accurate plots, the *Saladin* would have had little chance of reaching the convoy in time to assist in preventing the attack. She was detached at a distance of 30 miles, only 40 minutes before the attack took place.

Lieutenant Commander King approached the position of the burning wrecks at about 3:15 am. He saw what seemed to be a small object which, when illuminated by starshell, turned out to be the bows of an LST protruding about 15 feet out of the water with about 50 survivors on it. He went alongside, and took them off. There appeared to be a large number of survivors in the water all round, but as there were two or three power boats in the vicinity that had managed to get away, and the sea was flat calm, he considered it preferable to leave them to carry on with the rescue work and to wait until daylight before moving too close amongst survivors with the powerful screws at the stern of his ship. He continued to make an investigation of the area of attack, but found no E-boats.

By first light, reports showed that E-boats were returning to base and he requested permission to pick up survivors, which was granted. At 5 am LST 515 returned from the northeast and lowered all her boats to pick up survivors. *Saladin*'s commander thought it best to leave the job of picking up individuals from the water to the small boats while he screened the LST from further attack and searched for outlying groups of survivors. Whilst they were carrying out this duty the bow of another LST was found protruding out of the water about a mile to the north with two survivors on it.

As commanding officer of the Task Force, it fell to Rear Admiral Moon to interview the Royal Navy officers in charge of the ships concerned. He spoke first to Lieutenant Commander Geddes from HMS *Azalea* on 29 April. Admiral Moon first asked the officer what the picture was as he saw it.

Commander Geddes replied that when he left Plymouth he saw the *Scimitar* going into Plymouth and assumed that that was in order – that some arrangement had been made for them to go in there. He reported to the convoy commander and took the station he had.

Azalea came round to the area off Brixham where the LSTs came out and joined on. Coming around they came down on to the 206 course. Shortly after they got on to the 206 course the big advance of LSTs came along at about 3½ or 4 knots. The advance line of the convoy was in a single lane and very long. As an actual fact, he considered they were about three miles long. *Azalea* was about a mile ahead. Another thing he saw was somebody firing tracer bullets in the very rear of the convoy. Commander Geddes was thus just as concerned about the length and slowness of the convoy as some of his American counterparts that night.

A point not mentioned in his report immediately after the action was the wireless communication between LSTs. Throughout the whole time, *Azalea* never had any signals by wireless, or LSTs reporting, or any signals from the LSTs . She could have spoken to them by changing over to another wavelength, but that would have meant dropping one of her own lines.

Azalea was closing down to the convoy when someone opened fire with tracer bullets and the ship came around zig-zagging down the side. Commander Geddes intended to use star shells to illuminate the area at first, but there was doubt as to which side of the convoy was being attacked. In view of the length of the convoy, had he illuminated he felt he would have lighted up the remaining LSTs as targets if he picked on the wrong side.

Azalea, he told Admiral Moon, never had any radar contacts at all. When he came down the starboard side, he saw the fire and thought they were firing towards him. If they were firing at something between him and the convoy on the other side, he could not have picked them up at all. At that time the convoy seemed to turn to the northeastward and he remained astern of them all, zig-zagging across. Although they were all going to the northeast they were spreading over a wide front and he sent a signal to the *Tantaside* to alert her as to what was happening.

He received a signal back stating that other escorts were being detached, but no other escorts arrived. If another escort had arrived, Geddes was going to detail it to stand by the LSTs. By all instructions, he should have remained astern the convoy.

Admiral Moon asked him if he thought it was a little strange that he escorted the convoy with only one ship. He replied that he did. So the admiral asked whether he made any protest against proceeding? 'No, sir,' said the British officer.

'What is the usual escort for a convoy of this size?' asked Admiral Moon.

'It varies a lot, sir. Up until seven or eight weeks ago, I have been entirely on ocean escort, that is, running down to Cape Town, Algiers and such like from Londonderry and since coming down here, I have been in charge of coastal convoys.'

'Did you make any protest on taking this convoy with only one escort?'

'No, sir.'

'Did you arrange for radio communication circuits with the commanding officer or the convoy commander?'

'No, sir.'

'Did the convoy commander make any arrangements with you before departing port as to radio communications?'

'No sir, I joined the convoy in position after the convoy came out.'

'Would it have been possible for you to have gotten together before and made arrangements?'

'Yes sir, I think we could have made contact at the conference.'

'As to the question of radar, I want to find out if you received E-boat reports from the shore broadcasting stations.'

'We received them, and we were studying them when it started.'

'Did you actually see the E-boats themselves?'

'No, sir.'

Sonar contacts were reported in the same area and there was a possibility that there may have been a submarine. Admiral Moon asked about this, but Commander Geddes replied that he saw neither submarines nor E-boats throughout the action. He only got the one radar contact which he mentioned in his report. It was very close to the LSTs and he turned and headed toward it. But before he reached it, it disappeared. The HMS *Azalea* was fitted with a 4″ BL gun forward and a 2 pounder on the bridge. The admiral pointed out that there was a definite impression that there were two depth charges dropped in the vicinity very shortly before the E-boats made their appearance. This was the impression of several officers on one LST. But Commander Geddes assured him that *Azalea* did not drop any.

'Did you open fire at all?' asked Admiral Moon.

'No sir, I couldn't open fire because the target was alongside the LSTs and when I turned, if I fired my 2 pounder, it would have been at the LSTs which had not been illuminated.'

'How many survivors did you pick up?'

'I didn't pick up the survivors. When escorting we used to pick up survivors in convoy attacks right away. Since then we have had instructions not to pick up survivors until the actual attack is considered to be over. If I had had someone to assist I could have detailed them as a rescue ship. That is why I sent my signal to the *Tantaside*.'

Next, Admiral Moon spoke to the officer commanding HMS *Scimitar* that night. *Scimitar* was the ship which should have been with *Azalea* protecting the convoy, but was not.

'For some reason or other,' he began, 'you did not make convoy T-4. Will you inform me of the circumstances of that?'

Lieutenant Commander Shee, RN, replied that he arrived off Plymouth and received a signal from CinC Plymouth to go to number six buoy. He questioned the order and pointed out that he was supposed to be rendezvousing with a convoy outside. No one seemed to know. However, he obeyed orders and started there to have the damage repaired which he had suffered previously that morning from an LCI – Landing Craft (Infantry). LCI 324 had pulled out of the line putting a hole in *Scimitar* at about 00:45. Shee arrived at Plymouth and reported the damage, adding that the ship was satisfactory for sea provided there was no deterioration in the weather.

'Do you have a copy of the dispatch you sent?'

'I was in doubt about the signal telling me to go in and oil, so first of all I checked the address of it. The address was definitely for me. I queried it when I arrived alongside the oiler. The answer I got was that we had been told to come in by CinC and I suppose they had good reason for it.'

'What is your speed?'

'I can do about 26 [knots].'

'With your ship being damaged, could you have made your full speed?'

'I could have made full speed with the damage if it was in good weather.'

'How big was the hole?'

'About two feet wide and two feet long.'

'How far above the water line?'

'About 12 feet above the water line.'

'Did you send me any dispatch about your damage?'

'I didn't consider it serious enough to warrant and as I was returning to Plymouth I made the signal as a routine signal to inform them of the damage.'

The evidence taken by Rear Admiral Moon was passed up the line for assessment. It was the commander in chief at Plymouth, Admiral Leatham, who had to report to the naval commander, Western Tank Force, Admiral Kirk that the reasons for the absence of *Scimitar* or any relief for *Scimitar* lay in a series of mistakes and misunderstandings. Although the ship would have been seaworthy without repairs in the calm conditions prevailing the decision was made to keep her in harbour, and she was put on four hours' notice from 17:45 on 27 April. This decision was made without reference to the staff officer principally concerned, who was in fact under the impression that commander Force U and the senior officer, Escorts, were aware of the damage and had ordered *Scimitar* to return to Plymouth.

But it was not till 19:30 that the true situation began to become clear, and by then it was too late. In addition, to ensure that the right people knew at the right time, *Scimitar*'s signal at 10:15 on the 27th should have been addressed to commander Force U (R) CinC Plymouth and not repeated to commander Force U.

In Admiral Leatham's view, as expressed in a confidential memo written at the time, contributory factors were that the concurrent execution of Tiger meant urgent movements, planning and preparations. Exercise Fabius – the scheduled follow-up to Tiger – was close on its heels and compounded the problem. In addition, a night action with enemy destroyers was fought on the 25/26th and plans were made for offensive operations on 28 April. The capacity of his staff was severely stretched and the immense increase in communications caused abnormal delays in the distribution of signals. Finally, late distribution of the exercise orders and the incompleteness of some of the sets supplied gave very little time for their study and proper digestion by the many officers concerned.

But that was only the catalogue of things that had gone wrong before the convoy set out. Another Admiralty memo in my possession noted that no warning of the E-boats was received until the covering forces screen had already been penetrated. There was no radar contact until the E-boats were 10 miles inside their expected range. The shore plots were unable to keep pace with the many tracks in Lyme Bay, and while it was presumably clear that E-boats were operating in the eastern half of Lyme Bay, it was far from clear why convoy T-4 was allowed to steam right into the enemy. CinC Plymouth's orders were to go close inshore in case of attack. This was apparently construed as meaning actual contact with the enemy. Had the convoy been routed close inshore at the first warning there would have been a good chance of escaping the attack.

As it was, the E-boats were presented with an easy target, eight LSTs preceded by *Azalea*, the whole steaming in line ahead at 3½ knots. A destroyer on seaward bow or beam of the convoy might well have beaten off the E-boats. It had been done before on several occasions. But even allowing for only one escort, *Azalea* would surely have been better disposed on the seaward bow or beam and in a better position to defend the convoy and to use her radar free from side echoes from the LSTs.

Then, even once the attack was under way, the circumstances leading up to the loss of the LSTs were far from clear. A special chain of command was in force through the US commander. It was the same that would ultimately be used in Overlord. This arrangement in no way debarred the CinC from intervening if necessary, as he had said in his letter right at the outset of Operation Duck, to ensure the convoy steering a safe course.

A warning of the presence of E-boats was issued by the Cin C shortly after midnight. The convoy was attacked at about 2:10. There was no mention of any action being taken by the convoy in the intervening period.

It seemed clear the *Azalea* showed some lack of initiative in that action was not taken sufficiently early to keep the convoy clear of danger. It would seem that the ship took no steps whatever to avoid contact with the enemy after enemy reports had been received. It may be that *Azalea* was waiting for orders but that seems little excuse for steaming with nine ships in line ahead at 3½ knots towards the enemy for nearly two hours after the initial enemy reports. That she received these signals is stated in a letter from CinC Plymouth. But there was some doubt as to the relative responsibilities given to the senior officer of the escort by the senior US officer present. It was therefore decided not to attribute blame to the commanding officer of *Azalea*.

Full responsibility for the inadequate escort was accepted by Admiral Leatham. An extra ship, he admitted, might have made all the difference. But even while the staff officers were allocating blame and measuring any lessons learned for what they regarded as the 'real thing', the D-day invasion in two months' time, another – and unplanned – phase of Exercise Tiger was under way. What was to be done with the survivors? They knew that they had been on a rehearsal for Overlord. They knew that it had been a major fiasco. They would have at all costs to be kept from divulging what they had seen. The admirals might remember their mistakes, but the men who had taken part – survivors and dead alike – had quickly to be forgotten.

Ralph Greene was a captain in the US Army Medical Corps, serving in the lab of the 228th station hospital in Sherborne, Dorset. On the morning of 28 April 1944, Greene, like everyone else, assumed that the long-awaited invasion of France would take place soon. But while army trucks full of troops and supplies constantly passed by, and squadrons of aircraft ranged overhead, there seemed little for Greene and his fellow medics to do. That morning, however, the adjutant on the telephone had a distinct note of urgency in his voice: 'Colonel Kendall wants all officers to assemble at once.'

Within a few minutes, the unit's 40 medical officers and 80 nurses were gathered together. Colonel James Kendall, the regular army doctor who commanded the hospital, stood before them. Forty years later Ralph Greene can still recall his words. 'We're in the war now. In less than an hour, we'll receive hundreds of emergency cases of shock due to immersion, compounded by explosion wounds. Headquarters demands that we treat these soldiers as though we're veterinarians: you will ask no questions and take no histories. There will be no discussion. Following standard procedures, anyone who talks about the casualties, regardless of their severity, will be subject to court martial. No one will be allowed to leave our perimeter until further orders.'

Greene and the other doctors and nurses wondered what sort of secret operation might have gone wrong. Certainly something very strange was afoot. Their hospital compound was suddenly surrounded by a cordon of counterintelligence troops carrying rifles with fixed bayonets. Half an hour later a stream of ambulances and trucks began pouring through the entrance gates.

'They were all filled,' says Greene, 'with wet, shivering, blue skinned, blanketed and bandaged young Army and Navy men. Cold, wet and many in great pain, they were soon being treated inside the hut. Except for the medical personnel calling out to each other, there was no talking. The soldiers and sailors said nothing, and the doctors said nothing to them. Groans and sighs were all that marred the silence. Working in this weird vacuum, the doctors were gratified that most of the men responded quickly to warmth and TLC and that large numbers soon could be returned by truck to their units – whatever and wherever these might be. Many, however, responded less quickly, and despite every effort, some died. Meanwhile there was no explanation.'

Just as mysteriously as it had begun, the episode ended for the 228th hospital a few days later when all remaining patients were removed. Greene and the other hospital personnel did not know where they had gone, or why they had come in the first place. Soon rumours spread that many hundreds, perhaps thousands, of similar casualties had been sent to other hospitals. But there was no official acknowledgement.

This scenario was repeated in hospitals and casualty stations all over the southwest corner of England. Stanley Stout and the survivors with him were landed at Weymouth, and under armed guards with bayonets fixed were taken under strict security to a hospital and allowed no communication whatsoever with the outside world. While the wounded were being treated, they were very aware of the guards surrounding the building. True, Stout remembers, they were looked after very well by the doctors and nurses, but no communication was allowed with them, or with anyone else for that matter.

Shortly afterwards, they were moved several times more, each time further west until finally they were out in Wales – far away from the invasion areas. They stayed there for about a month and then men began to be shipped out to different units going into Europe. Within weeks they were all split up and sent in different directions.

When Arthur Victor and his comrades arrived in port they

were taken by truck to an Army hospital with the surviving soldiers, checked over physically, and put to bed. But they stayed there only a few hours. Next, they went to a Red Cross station and were given army fatigues, shoes and toilet articles. They slept there overnight. The following day they were taken to an Army base and counted in. Then the Army men went one way and the sailors went another.

After that, Victor and the others were moved again and housed in a dilapidated barracks, under guard, for three days, and ordered, under threat of court martial, not to discuss the incident with anyone outside their immediate group. At the end of the three days, they were sent by train to a Naval base somewhere in Wales and stayed there for five weeks, with one week being spent unloading an ammunition ship anchored well out in the harbour, and which they had to get to by boat. They were told – with no sense of irony – that this was a form of rehabilitation.

I have found no official documents relating to the treatment of the survivors, other than bland lists of the injuries they suffered. No mention was made of the way the units were split up, and many of the men found that when later in the war they told their comrades what had happened they were treated with suspicion and distrust. Equally, when – years later – relatives of those who had died tried to find out what had happened to their loved ones, they too met with a wall of silence. We shall return later to the question of what happened to the bodies of the dead, but it is worth noting one point here. Hundreds of bodies were seen floating in the water by the survivors, many were dumped unceremoniously in mass graves. But just a few were most carefully sought. Though Exercise Tiger is the story of the forgotten dead, there was a handful of officers that the Ministry of Defence could not afford to forget – at least until they were found and accounted for. These were the men who knew the secrets of the D-day landings. For the security services, the $64,000 question was: had the E-boats taken any prisoners and, if so, what did these prisoners know?

Ralph Ingersoll chronicled the history of the secret services during World War II. He relates how the TOP SECRET classification was reserved for those documents which contained the precise plans of the invasion, including the organisation of the assault waves and the arrangement of the supporting weapons – but neither the time nor the place where the actual invasion was to take place. This last information was reserved for still higher classification which was known as BIGOT. An officer who was entitled to, and did, know when and where the invasion would happen was known as a bigoted individual.

Amongst the officers and men who took part in Exercise Tiger there were a score or more of bigoted officers who knew the exact beaches on which the landings were to take place, and at what moon and what tide of what month. The Admiralty established that the convoy had been attacked while on its way to the beaches. So the troops would not have shared their officers' knowledge of what was to take place. Had the Germans happened on the convoy on its way back from the assault beaches, every GI on Exercise Tiger would have been worth sending to Berlin for interrogation.

But there remained the question of what had happened to the bigoted officers. Ingersoll was ordered to find out. He tracked down two lieutenants who had watched from the deck of the LST 289. The E-boat that attacked the vessel blew its stern off with the first torpedo, and then, according to Ingersoll's witnesses, hove to in the dark waters 100 yards away and turned on its searchlight. It played over the bobbing heads of the survivors struggling in the water. The E-boat cruised through the survivors and finally slipped away into the darkness. Obviously there had been plenty of opportunity for it to pick up survivors.

When this news got back, a whole day in Montgomery's headquarters was spent seriously contemplating alteration to the Overlord operation because of the knowledge the enemy must now be presumed to have. But, as Ingersoll recalls, by one of those amazing miracles which characterise war, although the bodies of hundreds who went down were never recovered, the remains of every single one of the bigoted officers was found. Each was recovered, its corpse floated by its Mae West, and properly identified. The tactics of D-day were secure.

But how were those few officers' bodies recovered, and not the corpses of the hundreds of ordinary soldiers and sailors? Clearly, someone must have sorted very carefully through the dead. But this implication of this question of the dead bodies was not one which I fully understood when I raised my Sherman tank from the sea at Torcross. Nor had I then heard any of the survivors' accounts which I have just related. It was only over the years between raising the tank from the seabed and having it dedicated as a memorial that I found out what I now know about Exercise Tiger. It was also during the same period that I met with many obstacles and heard from relatives and survivors of the difficulties which had been put in their path as they tried to find out the truth of what happened that night. The story of my discoveries really starts with my beachcombing at Torcross. But I shall begin by filling in some of the personal background details of Ken Small, the man who was walking along the beach that day.

6

EARLY DAYS

'My friends would have been very impressed if I had told them one day I would add a tank to my collection.'

I was born in Hull in 1930, of parents who were very poor. My father was an electrician, my brother an apprentice. My sister and I, she was a year and three months younger than me, spent most of our early days looking after my dad and my brother, because my mother was a very severe sufferer from rheumatoid arthritis, and spent a lot of time in hospital.

My first school was Endyke Lane Primary School in February Road, Hull. I was nine years of age when war was declared and it was not too long before Hull started to be on the receiving end of regular bombing raids and like everybody else we had to build an Anderson air raid shelter in our garden. Even as children we had to make ourselves useful to the war effort.

They were not easy times for any of us. My brother always used to complain because the cabbages he planted in our garden received a lot of hits from incendiary bombs. Then we used to get the so-called butterfly bombs, which would land and scatter anti-personnel mines all over the place. Once we had a direct hit on the house, when we were all down in the shelter. It did not destroy the house, but it did cause severe damage.

As children, we used to spend a lot of time away from school, and during the day we would often look at the sky and see the puffs of smoke that surrounded German aircraft as they flew through the anti-aircraft fire. The streets were usually littered with shrapnel and all sorts of bits and pieces of wreckage, which to children were great 'finds' to keep. There were two particular prizes I remember which were sought after. The Germans invented a huge land mine, which when be released from an aircraft would float down on a parachute. I remember one landing not far from us that stuck on a telephone pole. The mine itself was hanging only about eight feet from the ground, with the parachute entangled in the wires. If we children could get a piece of parachute webbing, or parachute silk, or cord, we felt great. To get a piece of a German aircraft was even better.

I remember on one occasion we heard of a German aircraft being shot down and a group of us went to the site. By the time we got there, it had been picked up out of the field, and was already loaded on an RAF lorry. It was being guarded by RAF personnel. Needless to say we ran under the back of the lorry and pulled pieces off that plane. You were really somebody if you got a piece of the plane, and if you got a piece with a number on it, any sort of number, that was the ultimate. How my friends then would have been impressed if they had known that one day I would add an entire tank to my collection! But when I look back, it seems that most of the time as children, we treated the war more as a game than anything serious, although I do well remember back doors being ripped from their hinges by people who needed to use them as stretchers to take out injured and dead from their homes. But children do not usually concentrate on the seriousness of the adult world.

The other memory from those days which sticks in my mind is the presence everywhere of the Americans. Of course what we wanted from Americans was what most people wanted – chewing gum and cigarettes. By this time, at the other end of the country, the people of the villages of the South Hams were being evacuated from their homes to make room for an exercise which would involve a large number of Americans. But to me then they were no more than a fine source of chewing gum.

After I had left school and started work, one thing did happen which I think throws some light on the character of Ken Small. In 1947, which was the worst winter on record at the time, we still lived in the village of Killingholme, and I had to travel three and a half miles to Habrough station before I could even catch a train to Grimsby, where I was working. The office was known to everyone as Fred Smith's Fish Merchants, but it was actually called Snowden and Woods. Fred Smith himself was a big, bombastic, bossy man, and his office manager was a Mr Boswell, who had an office just across the road from the factory. Getting to work that winter was a nightmare, and I struggled, I really did. The whole countryside was one white blanket – you did not know roads from ditches, or footpaths from fields. I struggled into the office, plodding through the snow every day. Throughout the whole of that 1947 winter I never missed a day at work; though sometimes I got in late because trains were virtually non-existent.

I remember getting into work on one particular day at about 12:30 in the afternoon. I walked exhausted into the office and the office manager told me Mr Smith had said that I had to go out again as soon as I arrived to fetch him an ounce of tobacco. I was wet through, I had holes in my shoes, water was soaking through to my skin, I was bitterly cold, and he wanted me to get this special tobacco. On top of all that, it was half-day closing and most of the shops had already shut for the afternoon. I tramped the streets of Grimsby looking for this tobacco, getting madder and madder and madder and not finding it. Eventually I went back and said to Mr Boswell the office manager that I wanted to hand in my cards. He contacted Mr Smith, who called me across to accept my notice.

Mr Smith is a man I never ever forgave, because he gave me a booklet. It was called 'The man who ignored the war' and basically it was about people giving in, surrendering being cowardly. I thought to myself, 'You swine, after all the times I have struggled to work, never missing a day in these atrocious conditions, always making it, and that was to be all my thanks.'

Many years later I had the opportunity to repay him. I had by that time joined the police force in Grimsby. After my initial training in Harrogate, I was put on the beat back in Grimsby. Being a probationary constable for a year, I had to go round and experience policing problems at first hand. By chance, I remembered the make of Fred Smith's car and the registration number OYR2. It was a Daimler, and Fred's OYR2 had parked in Freeman Street Market in Grimsby in a place where he should not have parked. This was my opportunity. I remember standing by that car for three and a half hours. Eventually he came up to me, typically cocky, and asked, 'Anything wrong officer?' 'Yes, sir,' said I, 'your car has been parked here an unreasonable amount of time.' Smith looked the picture of hurt innocence. 'Officer, I have only been 20 minutes.' With intense satisfaction I said, 'No, sir, you have been three and a half hours.' He was fined £25.00, which in those days was a considerable amount of money. It was such sweet revenge.

I wanted to make progress on the Grimsby Borough Police Force, but it was not to be. I did everything that could possibly be asked of me, but I soon found out Grimsby Borough were then the National Police Football Champions and to get anywhere on the Grimsby Borough Police, you had to be a footballer.

I remember one man, Barney Bircham, who came down for an interview. He played as goalkeeper, and he came straight out and said to the chief constable: 'Well it's like this, sir, I don't fancy walking the streets for 25 years.' The chief constable replied: 'Don't you worry about that Bircham, we have got men that can do that.' That really upset me. It meant in effect that walking the streets as a policeman was not a job, it was a punishment. If you were in another department like CID or the Warrant Office Department or the Traffic Department and you did something wrong, you were put on the beat as a punishment. Here I was living a life of punishment. So I said to myself there and then, that the first policeman I saw get promotion, who had less experience than me, would be my ticket off the Police Force. It was a Scotsman and he was a footballer, needless to say, PC Donovan. I left the Police Force almost immediately after that. It was a bitter moment, having done so well in my examinations. But I wanted to succeed because I was good at my job, not for some other totally unconnected reason, like ability at sport.

I had to think what I wanted to do with my life. As it

happened, while I was doing my police training I met Ann, my future wife. She was a hairdresser and was running a little business with her mother. They both worked very hard. After I left the police force, my wife's mother reminded me that I had once said that I might like to take up ladies hairdressing myself. Ann suggested that if I wanted to take it up I should go away and learn and come back and join her in the business. It was quite a move from being a policeman to being a hairdresser, but I did it, crazy as it seems, leaving my wife and mother-in-law to look after the shop and our two sons.

As it turned out, our hairdressing business was a success and I opened three more salons in outlying districts. Then came the rage for wigs, and I bought an old butcher's shop in the main shopping street in Grimsby with the intention of turning it into a wig boutique. I spent hours and hours studying this shop, which at the time still had sausage machines in the back, meat counters and hooks for hanging knives on, wondering how I was going to convert this into a wig boutique. But I did it, and we called it The Wigwam. When we opened, it received a lot of publicity on television, because it was the first one of its kind in the area. I remember my wife going down there on the first day we opened and she was still not home at eight o'clock that night. I rang her up and she said, 'Ken, I can't get the money in the till, it is literally overflowing.'

Then, quite by chance, the opportunity arose to move to Devon. We were sitting in the salon one evening, after a hard day, and Fay and Paul, one of my manageresses and her husband, suggested a holiday. So we all went down to Devon. I had never seen this part of the world; I thought all the English coastline was muddy like the North Sea. I had no idea that there was such beautiful scenery in England. The four of us were in Brixham very early one morning. It was pouring with rain and Paul, who knew the area better than I, was driving. Crossing on the Dartmouth Ferry, we did not stop until we found ourselves looking over Slapton Sands. It was quite the most beautiful view I had ever seen. It had then, and still has now, a mystery and a magic that drew me.

Later that year, Paul and I went down on our own for a

fishing holiday. We were so attracted by the place we could not imagine holidaying anywhere else. We were fishing just around the headland from the village and not catching much when I looked up and I saw this house. I thought how beautiful it was, and in a sort of idle way that it would be a nice house to live in. The next day I found out that it was a guesthouse, and when I saw someone water skiing in the bay, I thought it must be expensive to stay there. But when I had returned to Grimsby, a man from the village rang me up to say the guesthouse was on the market. I had been talking about how much I liked the look of it and word had got round. Two days later I went down again and bought it. I only spent a morning looking round. I spent a third of the time with the owner in the kitchen, a third of it on the beach looking out to sea and a third of it at Barclays Bank paying over a deposit.

We bought the house in January 1968, but we agreed the settlement date for September that year, because the lady who owned it wanted to carry on for the rest of that season. In September we moved down lock, stock and barrel from Grimsby, leaving some businesses under management and selling others. We spent from September to March trying to get it as we wanted it, as it was very run down, then we opened up as a guesthouse.

There was very little trade at first. The previous owner was apparently quite a rich lady, and if she wanted to close for a month she would take in no guests at all. There was only one family whom we 'inherited', and they said the only reason they had been suffering the place was because of the beautiful view. The food was atrocious, it was served late, and most of it was canned. The setting was to their satisfaction but nothing else. We were determined to be different. We had to make a success of it from the word go and we did and I am proud of the place, I love it. We were in the process of building up a success and I was in my seventh heaven. Not only was I running the guesthouse, I was fishing, I had crab and lobster pots out, and I even used to poach salmon out of the sea. Not any more, I hasten to add!

So there I was, a happy man, doing all sorts of fishing, and netting and potting, and running the guesthouse. Then all of a sudden, and I cannot remember the day, I got a severe bout of depression and had a complete nervous breakdown.

I had no reason for this breakdown. I had no financial problems, and at the time no personal problems either. I went to the doctor, several times, and to a psychiatrist. I took what seemed like massive does of Valium. I received weekly electric shock therapy at the hospital. It was a traumatic experience and I finished up having tearful days, verbally aggressive days, days when I hid away and did not do anything, and days when I did not want to know about fishing. I was interested in nothing at all. I was at my lowest ebb.

I have no idea why I suddenly went from being on a high down into the depths. I wish I could answer that. I had a successful business, I had a new car, I did not owe any money, the place was paid for, I had no mortgage. I had two boats, I had no personal problems, there was no reason at all. It just descended upon me like a cloud out of the sky. When I was down it was terrifying, that is the only word for it. I think there were many times when I felt life was just not worth living. It was not only traumatic for me of course but also for Ann and those who had to be around me. It is not something I would ever want to go through again.

It was at that time, when things were so bad, that Tony Steer came into the picture. He was the local fisherman who was to tell me of the existence of an unknown object offshore, an object that would turn out to be a tank. Tony came round one day and brought two pots and said: 'Come on Ken we are going out to check the odd pot.' I replied: 'No thank you Tony, I don't want to know.' His response was: 'We are bloody going,' and he dragged me out of the house. We went out and checked my pots. When we came back in, he looked down at the beach and said, 'Look at that down there.' I asked what he was talking about and he bent down and picked up an old threepenny bit. And then he told me about beachcombing. I took it up as a therapy.

I found while I was beachcombing, I was concentrating only on the beachcombing and not on anything else. Whatever problems I thought I had, beachcombing was all-absorbing.

The next thing I found might be a ten pence piece or an old half-crown. Next might be a gold ring, a gold coin, or a diamond ring. It was a constant delight. It took me over. It was through beachcombing that I got over my nervous breakdown, and it was through beachcombing that not only did I find the treasures of the beach, but also found out about the tragedies of this area.

This I think is one of the strangest parts of the whole saga of the tank. If I had not had the breakdown, none of this would ever have happened. It was the breakdown that brought Tony round and started me beachcombing. That led to him telling me about the tank. Without the breakdown, that tank would still be out there.

When I first took up beachcombing, and I was learning as I went along, I started to find coins, ordinary old coins, some very old, and a lot of jewellery, there were many thousands of pounds worth of jewellery. In those days, I would go out day after day after day. You can only beachcomb properly in January and February, because it was only then that the beach in these parts, which is fine shingle, will get sufficiently pounded. The sea is whipped up by a heavy easterly wind, and when the winds die down this results in an enormous swell rolling right up the beach. As the swell falls back to the sea, it pulls the shingle back with it. The beach level in 1974, the year I started beachcombing, dropped some 12 to 15 feet from what was known as normal. A lot of shingle had been washed out to sea and instead of walking on shingle, there was proper sand. The whole length of Slapton Sands, for that brief period, became literally Slapton Sands. Visitors have often said, 'Slapton Sands, where is the sand?' But in 1974 it was sand all right, so hardpacked was it that you could not have found a pebble on the beach and as you walked along even your feet did not make an imprint. The things I found – both military and otherwise – were not buried, they were lying on the surface. I did not use a metal detector to begin with. I used to wear thigh boots and warm clothing and I would walk along the edge of the tide as the sea came in and the swell rolled back. I had to be very quick, because as the swell rolled back it would reveal something – it might be bullets, it might be a gold ring, it might be a diamond ring – but I had to pick up whatever it was immediately, because the next swell would take it back again maybe never to be seen again. It was fascinating, and it was all-consuming.

I spent several years beachcombing along Slapton Sands, practically on my own. Then other people found out that I was finding things like the coins and rings and they started beachcombing too. When they began to bring metal detectors I realised I was going to have to get one as well. I remember my first metal detector very well. I went to Totnes to buy it. It was £80.00 and when I came back I did not go home. I went straight on the beach. Within five minutes I had found a gold bracelet which was then valued at £150.00. It had paid for my metal detector nearly twice over.

On one particular occasion when the beach was very firm sand, I found an enormous flat stone. I got a sounding underneath this stone and I tried lifting it but it was too heavy. I thought the sounding would only be a bit of scrap metal, but my curiosity was aroused. I went back and struggled again, but got nowhere. I left it again. But I had to get that stone up, I was sure there was something under it. As it turned out, it was a King Charles solid silver half-crown.

Then, in 1974, I had a series of quite spectacular finds. We had had a very severe storm. I recall it well because we were having extensive additions built onto our guesthouse, and somebody came in and said they had found a gold coin on the beach.

Up until that point, my finds had included thousands of ordinary coins, gold rings, signet rings and such like. But after this storm, I had not been able to get down to the beach, being tied up with work on the guesthouse. But on hearing about the gold coin, I went. It was quite late in the afternoon, still daylight, and rather strangely, it was the one and only time I went down to the area around the original monument the American Government had put up to thank the residents of the South Hams for evacuating their villages during the D-day rehearsals.

As I walked from the road towards the sea – away from the monument – I found that the waves had been so rough that about 20 yards out a huge valley had been sucked out of the sands. At the seaward end there was a high bank of shingle and the sea was coming over the top of this shingle bank and gently lapping to and fro at the bottom of the valley. The effect of all this was a sort of sifting out of the sand and the beach was so low it was down to coarse gravel. The first thing that happened was, as I was walking along, a policeman came over and said that I had better move away because there was a mine at the top of the beach and the bomb disposal people were going to blow it up. I was a bit annoyed, because I thought the beachcombing might be good with the sands so disturbed. I went to the bomb disposal team and asked how long they would be. They replied it would take them about 20 minutes, and as long as I was two or three hundred yards away, I would be all right. I walked away and watched from a distance as they probed the mine. Eventually, they moved away from it. I thought: 'Well, any minute now it is going to blow up.' Of course, when it did blow up there was a puff of smoke but no sound. It was only a second later that the sound came. Foolishly, I was startled by the noise and ducked my head. When I opened my eyes, right on the end of my toe, I found a 1308 Edward I gold coin.

I went a few steps further and found a Charles I gold coin, and as I went further, I started finding shrapnel, and a great deal of it. I also found another mine, which I must admit I covered up and did not report because the beachcombing was so good. I began to find different calibres of bullets and gold signet rings, along with shell cases and military buttons. I found a large petrol cap, obviously off a military vehicle. All this was near a monument which clearly stated that the American Government thanked the local people for getting out of the area during World War II.

The beach was covered with militaria. In this huge valley, dug out of the sand by the sea, there must have been tons of shrapnel and shell cases, live and spent bullets of all calibres, military buttons, bits of military vehicles, and pieces of piping.

My senses told me that something was not right. All I knew at that time was that men had lost their lives around the Torcross area during the war. I did not know how, or in what circumstances, or how many. So with this vague impression of unease in my mind, I tried to find out more. I spoke to several local people, and they all confirmed that men had been killed, but it was all rather ambiguous. The fact that any men at all had died seemed rather strange, because there was no monument to them at all, just the obelisk thanking the local people for getting out of their homes. And that monument was not put there by the Americans until 1954, which was 10 years after the event.

It plagued me – haunted me – as I carried on with my beachcombing. For weeks and weeks I knew something was wrong, but I just could not find out – or work out for myself – what it was. Until, that is, Tony Steer, my local fisherman friend whose family live nearby, told me of the existence of an 'object' as he described it some three quarters of a mile out at sea lying in 60 feet of water.

He also told me that during the war the whole bay had been full of ships, so that the River Dart was all but solid. You could walk from one side of the River Dart to the other, he said, without touching water. The area had many thousands of Americans staying in it, and that was why the local people were evacuated. Vast amounts of military equipment had been moved in and there was a rumour of a disaster out in the bay in which many men had lost their lives. No more than that was really known at that time.

Tony said that for many years trawlers had been snagging their nets on this wreck or whatever it was in the bay, and he suggested that he and I went out with a couple of divers to investigate. We went in my dory, a 13 footer. It was a calm day and the divers went down. We got all the usual blips on the sonar, but there was one much larger blip just in the area where we were looking. We dropped anchor over it and dragged an anchor along the sea bed. It hit something hard. We could not move the drag anchor any further, and as there were no rocks out in that part of the bay, we knew that it had to be what we were looking for.

Tony had a good fix of it on his Decca navigator, so the divers went down. When they came up, they told us that there was an American Sherman tank intact on the seabed, with its gun pointing in towards the shore. It was almost totally covered in trawl nets. We had expected to find a sunken ship on the seabed, but a tank was something else entirely. The divers went down again and they took off two very large front propellers from the tank. We could not be certain, but it seemed pretty clear that this was some sort of tank specially adapted for use at sea or in deep water. I took one of the propellers, which I have mounted on the wall in the guesthouse, and we gave one to the divers. Of course it was not very difficult to connect an American Sherman tank with something that must have gone on in the bay, and so I asked around locally.

Nobody knew about the tank itself but local people in the next village across did remember bombing and heavy shelling which they could hear even after they were evacuated. But what had happened was supposedly a secret.

It was at this stage that I thought how fantastic it would be if I could purchase the tank and recover it. When we came back from that first expedition it was more or less an instant decision that I should try and purchase the tank, salvage it and have it put on display as a memorial for the men who had died here. Within no more than a few days my mind was made up. I thought it would make a very apt memorial, even though I was not at all sure at that stage how many had died, or how, or why.

I did not tell anybody else about my plan. Once any wreck is known, it does very quickly become exploited by divers, so I kept my thoughts to myself for a long time. I did not even tell Tony, the man who told me of its existence in the first place, that I was launching out on a programme of purchasing the tank. I suppose from that stage on, I did not want to be thwarted.

I have often been asked why I decided that I wanted to buy the tank. After all, a lot of people if they found that there was a tank offshore, might think it interesting to dive down and have a look at it, but Ken Small wanted to buy it. I suppose part of it was that I had a gut feeling it simply had to be part of what I had discovered when I was beachcombing. Another reason I did not discuss the idea of buying the tank was that at that time I was a very private person. Of course I told my family, but their comments were not particularly enthusiastic. I suppose if you tell someone you are buying a Sherman tank on a seabed a mile out to sea, the initial reaction is you must be crackers. Nevertheless, my wife did not stop me. She could not have stopped me anyway, because it was something I really wanted to do. I just got on with it. These days when people come to the guesthouse, everybody talks about it, but it was very different then. The only publicity it received was one newspaper article. The *Sunday Mirror* heard about my efforts and they published an article. 'SOS Ken is caught in a tank trap.' The trap was the bureaucracy I was having to battle through to get ownership of this tank, but that was to come later.

Once I was involved with the tank, the nervous breakdown was not actually forgotten – you cannot forget that sort of thing – but it was very firmly put to one side.

The tank took over from the breakdown, the obsession over the tank, that is, recovering it and ensuring that it was brought ashore and dedicated as a memorial. Nobody else was prepared to help me, they backed off. But that only served to make me work at it the more.

More or less straight away, I started to find out more about what had happened back in 1944. I spoke to a man from Salcombe, called Richard Cove, who told me of a German E-boat attack. He was 16 or 17 years old at the time and he wanted to join the Home Guard or the LDV as it was known – the Land Defence Volunteers. We used to call them Look, Duck and Vanish. He was too young by a year, so he lied about his age and got in and worked on the shore batteries – there were two defending Salcombe Harbour. He was stationed on one of these shore batteries on the night of Exercise Tiger and he told me that his watch saw the silhouettes of the E-boats, but were instructed not to fire on them, because they did not want the Germans to know that Salcombe was a defended port. Actually, his exact words to me were that they probably would not have hit them, but they might have frightened them off. He told me of a substantial loss of life that night. But then again it was only rumour, and I had no way of confirming it.

It was only as the whole story unfolded that I began to find out exactly how many there were, and I began to hear from survivors. One in particular is Manny Rubin, an American who took part in Exercise Tiger and who now lives in England. He had met an English girl after the war and she went over to America. Then they found that he wanted to come back here, but his English wife wanted to stay in America. In the end, he won, and they moved back to this country, in fact to Devon. I met Manny very early on in my investigations about the tank, and he became an extremely dear friend. But when he heard about my plans to raise the tank his first reaction was to stop me. He has told me since that he was all ready to offer me a £1,000 not to do it, because of a fear of there being men's bodies still actually in it.

Manny and his wife used to visit Slapton Sands regularly and put flowers on the sea because he was a witness to the many hundreds of bodies floating around this area. He has never forgotten, and every now and again when he is asked to talk about it he breaks down and sometimes cannot even talk. Before I put up the tank as a memorial, he had nothing to identify with. None of the survivors and none of the relatives had anything to identify with. There was just a beautiful stretch of the South Devon coast with a deep blue sea, a fine beach, a main road and a large freshwater lake. It was just a twist of fate that the authorities decided that particular combination represented in detail Utah Beach in France, on which the troops were to land.

When I look back now so many things happened that I cannot explain, but that seem to have propelled me inevitably towards finding that tank and raising it as a memorial. One strange thing is that I suddenly decided to change the way I dressed. It was around the beachcombing time that I began to wear black, and I have never worn anything but black since. In fact my wardrobe is probably the most boring wardrobe on earth. I have nothing but black socks, black shoes, black sweaters, black coats, everything is black, shirts, ties, everything. The strange thing about this is that I never remember making the decision to wear black. I do not remember saying, 'I am going to go into wearing black because I like wearing black.' It just seemed to happen and it stayed with me from that day to this. Manny Rubin dubbed me 'The Black Saint'.

Then there is the series of coincidences surrounding the pendant which I wear round my neck. I have worn it for many years and it is featured in pictures in the lounge at the guesthouse and in our brochures. The reason why it is so important and attracts the attention of a lot of people is that it is made up of two particularly valuable pieces of jewellery which I have found. The ring top in the middle of it was not found with a metal detector. You have got to have a keen eye for that sort of thing, not anybody can do it. I picked it up, put it in my pocket, brought it home and we thought at first it was paste or diamante.

It stayed on the mantelpiece for months, then eventually I threw it among the less valuable pieces I had found on the beach, which I kept in a big copper fish kettle. The gold setting, which at that time I thought was brass, I put in an old tool box in the garage. A year or so after that a woman guest one Friday asked if she could look through what I called the less valuable material I had found. I dragged this heavy copper fish kettle out and put the whole lot onto a newspaper on the floor. She was looking through them when she found this ring top and said: 'Ken, I think these are diamonds. I said I was sure they were fakes but she was convinced they were real. She went to the bar, and she took an empty Coca-Cola bottle and scratched it. The diamonds cut into the glass. She left the next day, so I tried scratching the kitchen window, and again it cut the glass.

I took it to a friend of mine in Plymouth, Michael Cox, a gemologist. He put it on the counter, looked at it then looked at me, and told me it was a very valuable thing I had found. I asked what it was. He replied it was made up of ten Brazilian diamonds with an emerald set in platinum and a Georgian ring top. There was no shank to it, but on each end of it you could see a little gold coloured mark where originally a shank had been attached to the ring top. As for the surrounding piece, my young son found it in the tool box and brought it in and asked me what it was. I said it was a piece of brass I found on the beach. He said he wanted it and I said he could not have it. It turned out to be a 24 carat gold plate off a very old gold watch. So that was what made me put the pendant together, both pieces nearly thrown away, and both beach-combing treasures.

There is no doubt that I was obsessed, there is no other word for it. There was no reward in my mind other than to create a memorial to honour and respect the young men that had perished off this coast. There was no ambition for money, there was no ambition for publicity or anything other than to create that memorial. That was my obsession, that was my crusade. I would say I honestly believe I was given it to do by something I do not understand or someone I do not understand. I say that because I do not think I could have gone through the traumas of that very lengthy period without having such an obsession. It would have been impossible for one of my relatives or some fortune-seeker. They would have given up long before.

But now I had to buy the tank, gain proper ownership of it. I had formed the opinion, rightly or wrongly, that every wreck has an owner. You cannot just say there is a wreck out there and it is mine. That owner may be a government or an insurance company or a shipping firm. I had to determine ownership of the tank before I could buy it, and I did not want much to leak out because I wanted to go through with my plan to raise it as a memorial.

7

HOW TO BUY A TANK

'I rang my bank manager and asked for $50 to buy a tank.'

Having decided that I was going to buy the tank, I had to think what was the first step along the road. It was fascinating really, because I did not know where to start. How did I set about buying a tank, which was still out there under 60 feet of water, and the legal owner of which I did not know? What I did know was that I had to buy it. On an offchance, I thought I would ring the Customs and Excise office at Dartmouth and ask them if they could help me. The immediate reaction of the Customs and Excise was bewilderment. I doubt very much if they had ever had anybody ring them up and say that they wanted to buy a Sherman tank on the sea bed, and they were totally flabbergasted. On 30 October 1973, I had a short note back from them recommending that a good place to start might be the American Embassy in London.

They also enclosed a lengthy document from the Ministry of Transport, entitled 'Notes for Intending Salvors'. This stated, as I suspected, that all wrecks do belong to someone, and the first thing one had to do was make every effort to trace the owner. The document went on:

> Under Section 518 of the Merchant Shipping Act, 1894, and Section 72 of the Merchant Shipping Act, 1906, any wreck found or taken possession of and landed in the United Kingdom, whether recovered from within or outside the territorial limits, must be reported to the Receiver of Wrecks at the nearest Customs House. If the salvor is neither the owner nor operating by agreement with the underwriter or owner, such wreck must be delivered to the Receiver of the district. If no claim to ownership is

> established the Receiver will retain it for one year and, at the expiry of that time when it becomes vested in the Crown, sell it and make payment of salvage from the proceeds. In the circumstances mentioned in Section 522 of the Merchant Shipping Act, 1894, the Receiver has the power to sell wrecks in his custody at any time.

In other words, if I brought the tank ashore without owning it I was going to be in for a hard time. Clearly, I had to buy the tank before I brought it ashore. But knowing that got me no nearer to finding out how I should buy it.

I contacted the American Embassy in London. To be precise, I telephoned the Embassy. Most of my dealings were done on the telephone. Sensible replies were a little bit sparse in coming, and I had to keep pestering them, but eventually I got a response from the Embassy. Not that it seemed to move things very far forward at first. The US Army Assistant Military Attaché, Major James E Leonard, wrote that he was at a loss as to where to direct me to obtain ownership. He did say that he thought I should first contact my local authority and possibly the Department of the Environment, since he was unaware of the British legal position as far as my claim was concerned.

He also passed me on again. This time it was to the American Defence Supply Agency in Alexandria, Virginia, which was the office that controlled the disposal of US Government military property. This seemed to be just another link in the chain of red tape, but I telephoned the Defence Supply Agency and another round of letters and phone calls was under way. The Defence Supply Agency was in touch with the department of the Army to 'ascertain', as they put it, the legal status of the tank. One particular reply which made me laugh was sent in February 1974. The DSA said they regretted they could not consider the tank abandoned. This was a Sherman tank that had been down there under 60 feet of water in the English Channel for more than 30 years, and they could not consider it abandoned! What the letter did say, with some understatement, was that although the tank could not be considered as abandoned, it had been determined that demilitarisation requirements had been adequately covered by its immersion in salt water for 31 years. I do not think they really knew what to do.

They passed me on as well. They asked me to write to the Defence Property Disposal Service, European Region, in Wiesbaden, West Germany. This was the office which was dealing with the sale of military equipment in Europe, and which – they said – might be able to 'pass title of the tank to me by sale'. That sounded to me as though they might be able to sell me the tank, so I got on the telephone to Wiesbaden, and having been passed round several departments, I eventually made contact with Miss Sally Negata, who was to prove very helpful indeed.

I spoke to Miss Negata on the telephone and I wrote to her. I told her about the tank, and what I wanted and she was very pleasant and helpful. By April she was able to write back saying that a draft agreement had been prepared for me to obtain ownership title, although she was waiting for approval from headquarters to enable the agreement to be executed. In the meantime, they wanted to know what monetary amount I would offer for the tank. This was progress. In effect, she was saying I could have the tank, but we would have to agree what price I would be prepared to pay for it. I suggested £1. But she did not agree with that at all. She said that they needed to cover their administrative costs in drawing up the agreement, which they put at 50 dollars. So we agreed on a price of 50 dollars.

The whole thing took a long time, a lot of telephone calls, and a lot of pestering. I reckon they thought maybe if they left me alone for a while I might go away. But of course I had no intention of doing that, so it was telephone and telephone and telephone, just pressing them all the time for a response. In my mind, there was nothing but sheer determination that there was a tank out there and I wanted it for a memorial to those men. There was no way I was going to give up, and any red tape that was put in front of me as far as I was concerned was to be cut with a big pair of scissors. The pair of scissors in this case was me and my telephone.

Eventually, in July 1974, a draft agreement arrived, together with a contract of sale and a request for 50 dollars. The sale contract spoke of a Sherman tank (otherwise unidentified by either party) which I believed to be off the coast of Devon. I was buying something from them that they did not fully believe existed. There were also several clauses in that draft agreement which I found hard to believe. One was the position regarding any human remains, if there were any in the tank. In the agreement they said that in consideration of the fifty dollars the US would pass title over to me, provided that if I should discover any human remains on the said object, I would immediately notify the US Army Military System in Frankfurt and permit the US System to take custody of the remains. The contract further provided that if the said System determined that it had no interest in the remains, the said remains would be returned 'to the custody of Small and Small will accept custody of the remains with right of further disposition'. I have to say that I very much hoped no such remains were going to be found, let alone returned to me. Even in the annals of red tape, that does seem to be a little macabre to say the least.

They went on to say that I would not be obligated to demilitarise the tank because they considered that since it had been in salt water for 31 years it would have become demilitarised anyway. That seemed a blinding glimpse of the obvious. Another clause, in typical legalese, specified that if I ultimately determined that the object did not exist or if I determined that it does exist, but the US did not then have or never had any right or time or title in the precisely described object, nevertheless the US would be entitled to retain the monies thereto forthwith payable by Small.

So they would have kept the 50 dollars whatever. But I think probably the most amazing part of the agreement is this section:

> WHEREAS the US has no information concerning the existence and location of the tank, other than Small's letter of 14 December 1973, attached hereto and made a part hereof as Attachment A, and the US has no knowledge that it has or ever had any right or title to the said object as

> described by Small in said letter but is willing to transfer to Small any right or title, if any, it had or ever had in consideration of payment of 50 dollars by Small to US, providing that if Small should discover human remains this agreement is entered into and by the United States hereinafter the US and Kenneth Small hereinafter Small, The Cove House, Torcross, South Devon, England, whereas Small believes that a Sherman tank otherwise unidentified by either party lies in 60 feet of water located at a point approximately one mile due Northeast of the Cove House off the coast of South Devon, England and that it may have once been the property of The Military Department of the US.

I have since been told that I did not buy a tank at the time, I bought a piece of paper which entitled me to a tank, and I need not have paid for it at all. But that fact has only come to light in the last year or so. To say the least, there was a lot of red tape, and letters constantly passing to and fro. But my real dealings as regards the purchase of the tank were all thanks to Miss Negata.

I never met Sally Negata, even though she was a very important contact. Without her I honestly feel that I would never have got the tank, because there was a lot of opposition. I only wish I had met her. All I know is that she is of Japanese origin and she works for the American Government at that department. She was very obliging, in the letter I had from her after I had bought the tank, she wished me well with whatever I wanted to do. I have got the letter still.

In the meantime, I had to organise a cheque for 50 dollars. It seemed a very strange thing to do. I was a Devon innkeeper, not an international arms salesman, and I did not know if I could just start writing cheques payable to the American Government. So I rang my bank manager, Mr Garrett, and I asked if I could I have a cheque for 50 United States dollars because I was buying a tank. 'That's interesting, Mr Small,' he said. 'What sort of American water tank are you buying?' I said I was not buying a water tank, but a Sherman tank. The telephone then went very quiet. I suppose he could not believe what he was hearing. But to his great credit, I got my special cheque and I sent it off. Some time later I received the final contracts and agreements duly signed. But that was only after bureaucracy intervened again.

I thought I had the agreement of the Americans, but at the same time Her Majesty's Customs and Excise started to be less than helpful, because I had negotiated the agreement with Miss Negata and the US authorities, and pretty well ignored their various letters about salvage and value added tax. What I did not know at the time was that the Customs and Excise had seen a copy of my draft contract with the Americans. Their reaction was that there were several points which, to use their phrase, would deter the contract proceeding. In an internal memorandum, which is now in my possession, a Customs and Excise official lists five reasons. First, the tank would have to be demilitarised before it could be moved. This was despite the Americans having said that demilitarisation could reasonably be assumed to have taken place in 31 years of salt water. Second, only the American or British Government would be allowed to authorise the bringing of the tank ashore, or actually perform the salvage operation. Third, under English law they believed no private person would be allowed to purchase the tank, or rights in it, either before or after it came ashore. Fourth, only the Receiver of Wrecks could decide whom it belonged to. And fifth, a Coroner's Court would have to determine the cause of death of any occupants.

I was totally unaware of all these arguments being marshalled against me. But I was soon to find out. Just when I thought I was a very short way from getting the tank, in August 1974, I had a visit from Mr Vickers of RAF Molesworth.

Mr Vickers was an English civil servant working for the Defence Property Disposal Service of the American Air Force. Mr Vickers' exact words to me were: 'Mr Small what you do in this matter is entirely up to you, but as far as we are concerned it is extremely embarrassing because we did not know of this tank's existence. I must further inform you that I am going to the Receiver of Wrecks at Plymouth to recommend that the sale not be proceeded with.'

Of course, I asked him why and he produced a whole host of reasons, laid out in a document with the headings all listed neatly. It read:

1. PROBLEM: To determine whether to proceed with Negotiated Sale 50-5049-001 [the number of the contract I had from Miss Negata]
2. ASSUMPTIONS: The tank may not be US Forces material
3. FACTS BEARING ON PROBLEM:
(a) The tank could have been used by British, Canadian or US Forces during training exercises early in 1944.
(b) It is located approximately three quarters to one mile north east of Cove House Country Guest House, Torcross, inside UK territorial inshore waters.
(c) Coordination has been completed by DPDO Molesworth with HM Customs and Excise, The Board of Commissioners, and the Official Receiver of Wrecks.
(d) On-site verification of the location of the tank has been completed.
4. DISCUSSION: The problem is whether to proceed with negotiated sale 50-5049-001
(a) Course of action No. 1. – complete negotiations as established.
 (1) Advantages: None.
 (2) Disadvantages: Conflict with Host Country determination of procedures to be followed
(b) Course of action No. 2. Terminate negotiations.
 (1) Advantages
 (a) The recovery of the tank would revert to the British Government Agencies.
 (b) There would be no conflict with Host Country Agreements
 (c) If the tank was raised, the British Receiver of Wrecks and Coroner's Court would determine ownership and identity and disposition of any remains.
 (2) Disadvantages: None.
5. CONCLUSION: No official standing would be recognised of a unilateral transfer of 'rights' to Mr Small. Representatives

of Her Majesty's Government have stated policy that no private person would be allowed to purchase the tank or rights either before or after the tank had been brought ashore. Should at some time in the future, British Ministry of Defence raise the tank, and it proved to be US property, it would be so identified and offered for correct disposal. Any remains would have a Coroner's Findings to effect disposition. Demilitarisation in British terminology includes Delethalisation of any explosives which may be on board.
6. RECOMMENDATIONS: The course of action indicated in para 4b be approved.

Paragraph 4b was the paragraph which said negotiations should be terminated and I should not be allowed to buy the tank. Mr Vickers was a typical English civil servant. He was straight and to the point and official. Everything he did was done as is always done by civil servants. I suppose his job was to try and stop me buying the tank and he did it in the best way he could. He was short to medium height, a rather weighty man, with a moustache, the sort of man I expect to meet walking the floors in a department store. He was smart and well-dressed, the very opposite of me, because I have lapsed in my dress since I came down here. He was a nice enough man, he was polite, he was courteous, he did his job as he saw it and I accepted that. It was just that to me he was the instrument which was about to turn my dreams upside down. What he said made me feel quite sick before he actually went out of the door, and until I received confirmation from Sally Negata I got a sick feeling in my stomach that this might be the end of the two-and-a-half-year fight. I did not know at that time what influence Mr Vickers had, I did not know whether he was more powerful than Miss Negata or not.

As soon as Mr Vickers left and went off up the drive to the Receiver of Wrecks in Plymouth, I thought I had to ring Miss Negata. I called her in Germany and told her of Mr Vickers' visit and her comment was: 'Mr Small I told you you could have the tank, and you can have the tank, never mind what Mr Vickers says.' So I was to get the tank.

Mr Vickers meanwhile had basically decided, for whatever

reasons, that the best conclusion would be to terminate the agreement and that I would not be allowed to purchase the tank. He went to the Receiver of Wrecks in Plymouth as he said he was going to, and I received a letter from them to the effect that I would not be allowed to go ahead with the purchase. I also had a telephone call from a lady in the Ministry of Defence telling me that I could not have the tank, because no private individual in the United Kingdom was allowed to own or import a tank. Technically speaking I was importing it illegally, she said.

The letter from the Customs and Excise in Plymouth seemed very final. It read:

> Dear Mr Small,
>
> With further reference to your telephone call of Thursday last, following your meeting with Mr Vickers of the USAFE Defence Property Disposal Office, I spoke to Mr Vickers yesterday and understand that, after further consultations, they are withdrawing their offer to sell you the 'rights' in the Sherman tank lying off Torcross. He will be writing to you. This is a most unusual case and fraught with difficulties. It is feasible that it would be open to you to work it as a wreck. If so, of course, any landings of materials would have to be reported and delivered to the Receiver of Wrecks at the Customs House, Dartmouth. He would have to establish ownership and to decide as to potential liability to Duty and/or Value Added Tax. You would be entitled to a Salvage Award on any materials landed.
>
> Before any work was undertaken it would be necessary for you to contact the Command Diving Officer (Bomb Disposal Unit), HM Dockyard, Devonport for clearance – this is a safety measure.
>
> If any human remains were found in the Tank, the Police and the Coroner at Totnes would have to be consulted and their instructions complied with.

[This was a complete contradiction of the American idea on how the remains should be disposed of.]

> You are aware of course that the bringing ashore of the Tank would require a Licence, and landing of the guns, or any Small Arms that may be in the Tank, or any ammunition therein, would be subject to their immediate surrender to the appropriate authorities.
> Should you decide to proceed in this matter, perhaps you should care to call in and see me, when I should be glad to discuss the matter more fully.

The letter was signed by the Deputy Receiver of Wrecks at Plymouth. I just could not believe it. I thought yet again Mr Vickers had done as he said he would and recommended the sale not be proceeded with. In the nicest possible way this letter was more or less saying the same thing as Mr Vickers. They were putting a lot of problems in my way which might I suppose have put some people off again from going ahead. But it did not put me off. I decided to ignore the letter. I need not have bothered.

The letter from the Receiver of Wreck's office arrived on 14 August 1974. On 19 August I had a letter from Sally Negata in Wiesbaden, enclosing a formal contract for signature. This was not a draft, this was the real thing. The Americans were clearly aware of what the British were doing; they had seen the memos sent by the Customs and Excise, but they were going ahead with the sale in any case. I could not have asked for more. On 27 August, a fortnight later, I signed the agreement with Miss Negata. She countersigned it on 25 November 1974, and the agreement selling me my tank, the formal sale of government property by negotiated contract, was sent back after they had cleared my cheque for 50 dollars. Now I owned the tank.

I did not bother saying anything to the British. I was no longer concerned. I had possession of the tank and that was my prime concern. There would be no point if I started involving myself again with the British side of it. Had I done so, I think there would have been even more red tape and more complications. The Americans had sold me the tank. It was their property, and so as far as I was concerned, I owned it. After all, it was the Receiver of Wrecks in Dartmouth who recommended in the first place that I start trying to find out how to buy it from the American Embassy in London. I could put two piles of papers on my office floor, one a pile of papers from the Americans saying Yes and the other a pile of papers from the British saying No.

On the British side, it seems to me that we have a lot more red tape then the Americans do. I know the Americans have a lot of bureaucracy too. But in a recent comment, a colonel in the Pentagon said to me, 'Man, you have been up and down two great mounds of bureaucracy in the United States, you are halfway up the third, how the hell you have done it I don't know, but you have done it, it is sheer persistence.' I think probably if the English had been more involved in the tank, and of course it was not theirs anyway, I would have tried harder to counter any objections. But of course it was the American side that interested me most from the point of view of getting the tank, which was after all theirs, as a memorial to the men who died on this coast and offshore.

I suppose the moment when I really thought, 'It's mine,' was when I got the phone call from Miss Negata, when she squashed those comments of Mr Vickers, and said that I could have the tank. Once I had sent the cheque she was quite adamant about it. It was a wonderful feeling because it had taken nearly two and a half years to get hold of this tank, and it was a big relief that the waiting was finally over. I had also an immense sense of achievement.

The celebrations, such as they were, were quite muted. I had got over my nervous breakdown and had passed through that phase. I had worked hard to get what I wanted, but I just felt proud that I had become the owner of a Sherman tank, albeit on the seabed a mile offshore in 60 feet of water. I did not need a big celebration, I knew it was mine.

What was clear in my mind then was the idea of raising it as a memorial. That was very clear then in 1974, and it remained clear over many years, over the intervening years between finding the tank and recovering it. In fact, it was only about three or four years after I first thought about raising the tank that it suddenly occurred to me that 1984 was the 40th anniversary of D-day. From then on, I aimed for that date. It never occurred to me to give up, never.

It would be many more years before my dream was realised, and there would be a lot more 'Mr Vickerses' along the way. But at least the first stage of my crusade was over.

8

THE RECOVERY BEGINS

'There were two boats, the diving vessel and the fishing vessel, bringing my tank ashore.'

In November 1974, even if I did not know all the details of Exercise Tiger that I have related, I knew that there had been a great loss of life. It was only over the next ten years, as I worked to salvage the tank from the seabed, and then have it properly dedicated, that the full story was to unfold. When I look back now, it seems that the more I found out about Exercise Tiger, the more I knew that what I was doing was right, and that it had to be done. The image of those men in the dark waters of the English Channel was enough to spur me on.

But enthusiastic as I was, I realised that I could not just start pulling the tank out of the sea straight away. I had not yet thought through in detail what would be involved in a task of that size and complexity.

Obviously, I had not tackled anything like this before, and when I think back to those early days everything seems so insecure and uncertain. Indeed a couple of years later, just when I thought the nightmare of red tape surrounding the purchase of the tank was well and truly over, a man phoned me and said that the tank was not in fact mine but properly belonged to him. I could hardly believe what I was hearing. Surely all the troubles with the Receiver of Wrecks were not about to start again. I asked him to explain himself. He said he had bought the recovery rights to all military equipment in the South Hams area from the US Government. It seemed a cast iron case. My instant reaction was panic, but I did have the good sense to refer back to my agreement. I asked him when he had obtained his rights. He replied that he had concluded his negotiations with the American authorities in that year, 1976. With great relief I realised that my agreement easily pre-dated that by two years. I was safe. When I pointed this out, his only comment was, 'That's rather naughty of them,' referring to the Americans.

Having got that shock out of the way, I was free to pursue my dream, for it seemed not much more than a dream at the time. There was not a great deal of money in the guesthouse. True, we were making a reasonable profit, but all the money we had was tied up in the guesthouse. I knew a salvage operation was going to be expensive, but all I could do was hope for help. During those early years, I had to plan the whole project in my own mind. Like it or not, I had to work on the basis that in the final analysis it would probably all be down to me and me alone.

The first real step along the road had been the thought that it would be nice to recover the tank in time for the 40th anniversary of D-day, which was 6 June 1984. That gave me no less than 10 years in which to work. Having come to that initial conclusion, I made a plan that I would recover it on that very day. Still, I did not know where to start, so I looked in the Yellow Pages of the telephone directory. I looked under the heading of Diving Firms, and started to make my phone calls. I got promises of help from countless different firms, but that was all they were, promises. One by one, they all came to nothing.

The reaction of the diving firms I contacted, not just the one I eventually dealt with but all of them, tended to be much the same. When I explained to them what I wanted to do, to raise a tank off the sea bed, their immediate response was to say that they wanted to be involved. Some even offered to work for free, because of the publicity it would bring their firms. But each one I contacted eventually dropped out. Usually, they gave no reason. I suspect that on second thoughts, they realised it was a bit too much of a task for them to tackle. The whole thing was a bit too complicated. It sounds very nice to lift a 32 ton tank off the seabed, but in practice it is a very difficult operation.

At the same time, I thought I should enlist American help.

After all, the Americans had in the end been very cooperative when it came to buying the tank. So once again I contacted the Embassy in London. This time, they referred me to the officer commanding one of their big bases at Mildenhall in Suffolk. I tried on a number of occasions to contact this man, but I did not get any response.

I rang back to the Embassy again and spoke to my contact. He was less than helpful. He said that what I was doing was a private responsibility, and that the American Government did not get involved in matters of that kind. My reply to him was that it was far from being a private responsibility to order those young men to give up their lives. It was official, and there should be some official recognition of the fact. By this time I was really annoyed, and I put the phone down on him. Within an hour, I had a phone call from the officer commanding Mildenhall saying that they could not help because the American military had no equipment in England with which to assist in such a recovery, the nearest being miles away on the continent of Europe. So that firmly squashed any prospect of American help in the recovery.

My next thought was to turn to the British Army for assistance. Through a chance meeting, I had spoken to Colonel Dick, who lived not far away in Dartmouth and worked in the Ministry of Defence. He had casually mentioned that if he could be of any assistance to me over this recovery, he would do his best to help. Matters were getting a bit desperate, so I decided that I would try and contact him. I rang his home in Dartmouth and was told he was not there but could be contacted at his office in the Ministry.

I rang there and spoke to a young woman on the switchboard, and asked if I could speak to Colonel Dick. She politely but firmly corrected me and told me that Colonel Dick was now Brigadier Dick. To my mind this sounded like a definite step in the right direction. If he was one rank up, he would be more able to help. When I was put through to Brigadier Dick, it certainly seemed that way. He was fully co-operative and clearly very enthusiastic about the whole project. Through his intervention, it was arranged that the Army would become involved in the recovery as an exercise. It would after all provide them with practice at heavy recovery, and make for good publicity at the same time. Brigadier Dick's proposal was that the Army would take over from the point where the tank was deposited on the beach or within 100 or so yards of the shore. The soldiers would be able to move it up the final stages to a ramp or plinth which would be prepared for it, though, at that stage, I had not even finalised exactly where the tank was going to be positioned. All the same, the organisation went ahead and some officers and Marines came down to Torcross to have a look round, and I had a visit from a captain in the Third Royal Tank Regiment, David Cowley, who arrived with his corporal to act as a sort of co-ordinator.

But even though all seemed to be going well, it was only a small part of the project. What I had arranged so far was only the process of getting the tank from the beach to the plinth. I had wanted American help in getting it from where it was on the seabed onto the beach, but that had been denied me. So I still had to find someone to help with the offshore and underwater side of things. Eventually, I contacted a firm of divers in Plymouth who did seem to be able and willing to help. It was decided that there would be two diving instructors involved and a number of trainees. Again it would offer good practice for them, while at the same time solving my problem. The instructors were Bill Doughty and Peter Panades, and they would work with one salvage vessel and 12 trainee divers. They reckoned they could take on the whole of the seaward part of the recovery and the firm sent me an estimate for the work, which I accepted.

There had to be a considerable amount of planning as to how exactly we were going to go about the operation. I did not know much about recovery techniques and I remember at the time I had several sheets of paper on my desk with countless places that I had phoned and ideas that had been given to me. But the one that finally came up as the best way to recover the tank would be to attach six flotation bags in sets of three pairs, joined together under the front, the middle and the rear of the tank. Each pair of bags would be joined together by a very thick nylon strop. The idea of using nylon was to prevent any damage to the tank. The bags were to be taken down to the seabed and attached to the tank and then inflated from a surface salvage vessel by compressed air. Hopefully the buoyancy of the bags would break the suction that was holding the tank to the seabed and lift it into the water.

Each bag had a lifting capability of 10 tons, which made a maximum lifting capability of 60 tons. The tank we knew weighed 32 tons, and we calculated that it would have about 8 tons of silt inside, which made a total of 40 tons. But what we could not be certain of was the degree of force that also had to be taken into account to break the suction off the seabed. The tracks were not buried, but the tank was firmly embedded on the bottom. All the same, the flotation bags seemed obviously the best idea and indeed it turned out to be so.

I have nothing but praise for the way the divers worked, but I am afraid the same cannot be said of the firm they worked for. I will not name the firm here; I am not about to give them free publicity, but I have to say that their estimate did not work out as I had hoped or expected. It was in the order of £3,000 for the whole job, but that included £800 for the hire of the six large flotation bags, which would be used to raise the tank to a midwater position before it was towed ashore. The firm which was to provide the flotation bags was called Halt Marine, based in Norfolk and its proprietor was called John Wise. £3,000 was a lot of money to me at the time, so I thought I would contact John Wise and tell him what I was doing, and see whether this relatively large part of the bill could be reduced. I rang him up at his firm in Norfolk and told him what was happening. Considering that I was just phoning up out of the blue he was very helpful. Once he understood the cause for which I was working, and the reasons for bringing up the tank, he said that I could have the bags on free loan, which was a saving of £800. Or so I thought. Unfortunately, it did not quite work out like that. While I can hold out nothing but praise for the instructors and the divers who worked on the recovery, because they really did work hard, when it came to the directors' office, things were slightly different. When the bill came in, it took no account of the deduction of the £800 that I had managed to arrange by negotiating the free loan of the bags. I raised this with one of the directors of the firm and he got very annoyed on the phone, and told me that what I had originally been sent was only an estimate. The £800 had gone to all the extra work involved, and if I wanted he would send me in a much much bigger bill, because estimates do not carry any legal backing. Frankly, this frightened me and I paid up. But I was not very pleased, because it was all in a very good cause and after all they were using the project as a training exercise for their divers. They had an opportunity to be involved in a unique recovery operation which was a fine opportunity for the trainees, and for that matter for the instructors, because experienced as they were, they had never recovered a tank before.

Some time in February 1984, I started to think that I really would soon be able to bring the tank ashore. The preparations for bringing all the teams down to Torcross, and physically getting everybody together, were all completed. I never wrote a single letter throughout that whole period. Like so much of this whole project, the organisation was done almost totally on the telephone.

We were getting to the point where recovery could start. But in the letter I had received from the Customs and Excise, it was stipulated that before recovery got under way the Royal Navy should spend time on the tank (or the wreck as they insisted on calling it) to check it for dangerous ammunition or explosives. I had to organise that side of things carefully. I got in touch with the command diving officer in Devonport and explained what I wanted to do. The Navy were very helpful, and the result was that HMS *Datchet*, a Navy diving vessel, was brought to Dartmouth, with its captain and crew of divers. Getting the Navy involved was one part of the whole process which presented no problem, perhaps because that was more or less a legal formality. Whatever the reason, they did what had to be done and were extremely co-operative. It was the spring of 1984 when the recovery could really be said to have started. That was when the first Navy team arrived. I was told that the team would soon arrive in Dartmouth and would I join their vessel at Dartmouth harbour. I went aboard the diving tender HMS *Datchet*, was greeted by the captain and the crew and we set out from Dartmouth harbour. The operation was under way. After searching with the echo-sounder, we found the location of the tank.

I should mention here that finding the tank was rather easier said than done. Each time we went out during the time we were making preparations for the recovery, we had to comb the area with an echo-sounder. Eventually we finished up with an echo chart with a little blip on it which indicated the actual position of the tank on the seabed. That was found with sonar, taken at normal speed, drifting back over the tank at 2 to 3 knots. But it would be very inconvenient if we had to keep taking sonar readings every time we went out. So having located it we took land co-ordinates to line up on. A tank may seem big on land, but on the bottom of the sea it is no more than a tiny speck. Our bearings were a fine mixture of nautical precision and local geography. We had a chart which pinpointed Stokeley Manor, which is a local manor house, at 292 degrees, the local hotel at 260 degrees, the lighthouse at 200 degrees, and the American monument at 352 degrees. To be certain, we had to line up a whole series of local buildings. Cliff House had to be in line with Greyhomes, Widewell Barn with the Crowing Cock, and Rews Wood with my friend Reg's house. I told all this to the Navy team who were amused and impressed. At least we knew how to find the tank easily.

HMS *Datchet* dropped anchor over the tank, and they made their preparations for the first dive. Actually it was quite a social occasion, because I had never been on a Navy ship before and these men were absolutely first-class company. I always cast myself as being susceptible to sea-sickness, but fortunately it stayed calm and they fed me well. They had a way of cooking which I had never seen before in my life, despite having spent a lot of time in the kitchen of the guesthouse. There was a large soup bowl, permanently on the go aboard this vessel. What they did was to fill it with anything and everything that came out of their ration tins, whether it was meat, beans, carrots, onions or potatoes. They would just shove the whole lot in out of these tins and stew it up. We would all eat this stew with great big chunks of bread. But the next day they did not empty the pot, they just added more and more tins. This went on for the whole period they were diving on the tank. It may not sound terribly appetising, but it was wonderful food. They were also a superb team of divers.

Their job was to go down and examine it and try to establish whether there was any dangerous ammunition or explosives on board. The first few times the divers went down, in addition to checking for explosives, they had to use suction pumps to clear out at least some of the silt that had built up over the years. In addition, before they could get inside the tank, they had to clear a considerable number of trawl nets. Over the years, fishing trawlers in the bay had constantly snagged their nets on the tank. It had ripped great holes in their trawls and most of the netting had settled down on top of the tank like a shroud. Forty years of trawl nets were entangled on the tank, so the Navy spent quite a long time trying to cut them away. They never did succeed in getting rid of all the netting, but they did clear most of it.

Then, when the divers from HMS *Datchet* were just about ready to get into the tank through the hatches, we hit an unexpected problem. On this particular dive, they were not down very long, and came up looking rather shaken. They had come across a group of extremely large conger eels, which had taken up residence inside the tank.

One of these eels was in excess of 80 pounds weight. The divers were from the Bomb Disposal service, and no one could ever doubt their courage, but their reaction to the conger eels was quite firm. As one of them put it: 'We are not bloody going in there with those things down there.' We had to dispose of these eels. So discreetly they took down thunder flashes and set them off. Some of the eels must have been killed, others were frightened away. It was unfortunate but it had to be done; the safety of the divers came first. Once the uninvited guests were out of the way they dived on the tank for three days. Each night I went back to port, hoping that they would not find anything too serious in the way of explosives, or – worse still – human remains, though I was fairly sure that all the crew of the tank would have evacuated safely when it went into the water.

As it turned out, no explosives or human remains were found. The tank was in quite a state when they first dived on it, and they worked well to clear it of so much of the silt and the netting. As the third day progressed, it was clear that they would soon be finished, which meant that the main team of salvage divers could get to work. I had organised things so that the salvage vessel should take over immediately the Navy finished. So at one stage the Navy tender and the salvage vessel were both there on station at the same time. When the moment came, I stepped off HMS *Datchet* and onto the salvage boat. The Navy returned to their normal duties, but they did have one mild word of warning. Although they had not been able to find any dangerous ammunition or explosives, they felt that in view of the vast amount of silt still in the tank they would have to give it another inspection once it reached the beach, if it ever did.

At this stage, I was, for want of a better word, co-ordinating all the separate groups who were involved. We had the Navy, we had our own team of divers, and we had the Army. Set down like that, it sounds like a recipe for chaos, and it was chaos. But being of the nature that I am, once I decided that this project was going to happen, I devoted my whole mind to it.

I thought about it every day, when I went to bed at night, and as soon as I woke up in the morning. I spent hours and hours, days, weeks, and months getting everything organised and eventually I managed to do it. I had no real help in the organisation, I had to do it all myself. As for fixing the actual time and date when it was all going to take place, I cannot really remember how that came about. I wanted the tank up for the 40th anniversary of D-day, 6 June 1984, and that was my only goal. I was determined to have it up on its plinth before that day. The recovery team had given me an approximate idea of how long it would take them, but I did not know how long the Navy were going to take.

When they all came down, there was not room for everybody in the guesthouse, which was probably just as well.

The way it turned out was that the Navy team were aboard their ship, and so were the salvage team aboard theirs. All the divers lived on board ship. They worked in shifts to get the tank up as quickly as possible in case the weather changed. But I still had a lot of people here during the actual recovery. In particular there was a host of journalists, reporters and photographers. Each evening we would gather in the bar of the guesthouse and I would wine them and dine them free of charge.

With their work completed at least for the time being, the Navy took their leave, and the salvage vessel took over. The first part of their operation was to go down and clear the rest of the trawl nets. The divers were not students, but trainees. Their firm actually trained divers for difficult tasks, like working on North Sea oil rigs. I cannot stress too much the careful and very intricate way in which the diving instructors carried out their duties with the trainees. Everything but everything was checked. I noticed that both the naval and civilian divers had exactly the same routine at the start of the day. They would gather round in a circle and the officer in command if it was the naval team, or the instructor in charge of the salvage team, would give a thorough briefing. Each little detail was discussed in great detail. Obviously, safety was uppermost in everyone's mind.

If anything had gone wrong, the Navy had decompression chambers on board their vessel, but the salvage vessel did not. So there was a smaller margin for error once the Navy had left, although we knew that we could very quickly summon assistance if we needed it. The divers went down in teams and cleared the remaining trawl nets off and attached the flotation bags to the tank by passing the nylon strops underneath it. That was undoubtedly one of the most difficult parts of the whole operation.

The tank was very firmly embedded in the sand, so they had to scoop away a channel under the tracks and then pass the nylon strops beneath the tank, under both pairs of tracks, and out at the sides. Then they had to attach the flotation bags in three sets of two. The idea was that the bags would be inflated once they were in position. But setting them in place was a painstakingly slow process. Bags kept on breaking free just as they were almost fixed, and floating away into the bay. The visibility in the water was not all that good and the current was strong, so that every time a bag escaped it was a fairly major exercise to replace it.

It was three days before the bags were successfully attached and in their positions ready to be inflated. They switched on the compressed air pumps on the deck of the salvage vessel and pumped air down into the bags. They started to inflate, but still the problems were not over. Again bags kept on breaking free, because they had not been secured firmly enough. Each time a bag broke free it would shoot up to the surface with a great rush of escaping air, and the divers had to go down and fix another one in place all over again. Then once the first successful inflation of the bags was completed and they started to take the strain of the weight of the tank, the nylon strops between the three sets of flotation bags snapped.

The nylon was woven into a very thick sort of rope, but it was simply not strong enough. The whole idea of using nylon was to prevent the bags and the tank from being damaged. But we would have to think again.

The divers discussed this with me and said it looked as though they would have to use heavy metal strops. I agreed. But that meant yet again going through the process of attaching the bags. This time, they had to be attached to the ends of three metal strops. Then inflation started again. But still we were not quite there. Several times the tank was lifted off the seabed only to be lowered again. The strops moved from their proper positions. A bag deflated. It seemed to be going on for ever.

Eventually they succeeded and the tank was lifted from the seabed. As luck would have it, I was not on board the vessel when they finally made the successful lift. It was evening, and I was at home in my dining room, looking out to sea. I could see the lights of the salvage vessel and of a local fisherman who had his boat out there to assist with the recovery if need be. I remember the occasion perfectly, the dining room was full of photographers and journalists and we were all sitting round talking.

I was looking out at this small flotilla of lights constantly throughout that evening. Each time, I lined up the lights with some rocks on the shore. Then suddenly I saw that the group of lights was slowly moving through the darkness. They no longer lined up on the rocks where I had been looking a moment before. The whole assembly was inching towards the beach. The thrill was incredible. There were the two boats, the diving vessel and the fishing vessel, bringing my tank ashore. It needed the two of them, because they were towing some 40 tons in middle water, roughly about 30 feet from the bottom and 30 feet from the surface.

I just dropped everything; we all did, and ran down to the beach and watched as the little convoy approached. When they were quite close inshore, they lowered the tank, still out of sight in about 25 to 30 feet of water, and about 150 yards off the beach.

It was one magnificent sight, it really was. It was a sight for cheers and jubilation and whoops of joy. The tank was coming ashore. But by now it was late evening, so we left it in that state until the following morning.

The day of the recovery would be day five of the operation. The tank had arrived at the beach, or at least within easy reach of the beach, and the salvage vessel's job was done. It stood offshore for several hours and then pulled away. Now was the time for the winching to start. It seemed that everything was ready to bring the tank ashore. The only minor snag was that when they had brought it inshore and lowered it, they did not realise until too late that it had not settled properly onto its tracks, but had slid partly onto its side. Fortunately, a local plant hire firm, Richard Cummins, offered their equipment free of charge. They sent one of their bulldozers and attached a cable to it. The bulldozer stood parallel to the beach with the cable fixed in place and ready to pull the tank to a fully upright position before the process of winching it across the beach began.

With the tank still on its side, it took the strain. It worked, and we soon had the tank sitting properly on its tracks. The next step was for the bulldozer to be used as an anchor point on the beach for the main winching operation. But the winching was now a problem. I had been given to understand that the Army were going to effect the winching programme, although, as it happened, a man called Tony Gregory, who had a winching firm in Cornwall, had contacted me. He had heard about the story in the local papers and said he would be willing to stand by with his winch vehicle and assist if necessary, free of charge. The way things turned out, it was just as well.

Just as everything seemed to be set, the Army pulled out. It happened completely without warning. One moment I was expecting them to help, indeed play the major part, in moving the tank up the beach, the next I got word that they would take no part at all. I had my tank almost ashore, but no way of finishing the job.

9

ASHORE AT LAST

'In that case, you don't bloody well need the Army.'

On the Monday before the tank was due to be recovered, I had a call from Major Gudgeon in the Ministry of Defence and his assistant, Martin Helm. They said that the Army were no longer interested in the project and would not help in the matter. I asked Major Gudgeon to explain this complete change of attitude. His response was first that it had not gone through the proper channels – this was despite the fact that I had arranged everything as high as brigadier level – and second, if the Army failed in the exercise it would mean bringing in massive recovery equipment. That in turn was something which would require special dispensation from the police and I would have to bear the full cost. This line of argument was completely at variance with what Captain Cowley and the other experts on the spot had said. In their view, there would be no need for massive recovery equipment. But this argument was lost on these gentlemen with the crowns on their shoulders sitting in their offices with their cups of coffee. I told the major I was sure we would not have to go to the expense of bringing in extra heavy lifting equipment, because there was a man in Cornwall willing to stand by with his heavy winch vehicle to assist if necessary for no fee. Major Gudgeon's reply to that was: 'Mr Small, in that case you don't bloody well need the Army.' With that he put down the phone.

So it was that Tony Gregory carried out the whole winching programme with his vehicle, though he was not entirely on his own. He had the assistance of two local engineers, Jim Perrot and Gerry Weymouth. What is even more ironic is that when he turned up, the vehicle he produced on site was a vehicle he had constructed from ex-Army equipment.

The divers went out and attached cables to the tank. Initially, they snapped off at the point of connection, because the eyes onto which they had been fixed were corroded. The divers found a much stronger fixing point underneath the front of the tank and attached the cable. By this stage hundreds of people were watching. They had been watching over the whole period of recovery, everybody hoping the tank would come ashore on a day when they were in Torcross. But we could not run to schedule quite like that, because of things going wrong. The engineers and the local people, Jim Perrot and Gerry Weymouth, were in their overalls and waist high in the sea by now. The enthusiasm of this handful of local volunteers was incredible. But it did all seem to be taking an awfully long time. And although the firm of Richard Cummins lent the plant free of charge, I think even they were getting a bit concerned about the amount of time their foreman was spending on the project.

The local electrician and almost everybody else who lived in Torcross were there. It was a marvellous local effort. Chris Venmore, the fisherman, Jimmy Simmons, the bulldozer-driver, Jim Perrot, Gerry Weymouth, and countless others, all worked together. The attitude was: 'Come on, let's give Ken a hand to get this damn tank out.' I remember I was worried sick because the bills were mounting as it was delayed. I used to ask them if everything was going to be all right. I always got the same reply, 'No problem, no problem.' If they said that once they said it hundreds of times.

Slowly they started winching the tank ashore. All we could see at that point were two of the large flotation bags, the others were trapped under the tank. We still could not see the tank itself. They had to winch it for a time then pause, because the winch vehicle was on the main road and every now and again the cable had to be lowered to allow traffic to pass.

When the tank first appeared, there was a strange noise, a sort of extremely heavy breathing noise, as it loomed up out of the water – intact. It was literally half inch by half inch as it came slowly out of the waves. Eventually, it reached the point where it was all free of the sea except the tracks, and the divers took me out in their inflatable dinghy to welcome my tank ashore.

I had a very old bottle of champagne in the guesthouse – I had had it for years. It had to be cracked on the tank. So they helped me aboard the tank, which was slippery, and I climbed up onto the top of the turret. There was a huge crowd of people there, and numerous pressmen lined as they do, with the first row on their knees, the second row standing up behind them. Everyone was waiting for me to welcome the tank ashore with my bottle of champagne. I made one almighty throw at the tank with the champagne bottle but much to my astonishment and embarrassment, it bounced off. It went curving into the sea and disappeared from sight under the water. There was a pause, then one of the divers, I think it was Bill Doughty's son, recovered the bottle from the seabed and brought it back up to me. I was more careful the second time, and I was successful. I smashed the bottle of champagne on the top of the tank and a wonderful cheer went up.

I got back on the dinghy and came ashore and the winching slowly continued. The anchor point of one bulldozer proved totally inadequate; it started to tip up slowly until it was nearly standing on its head. So we had to bring in another even bigger bulldozer and the two were chained together to form the anchor point. Tony Gregory told me that at this point his winch vehicle was pulling the equivalent of 400 tons. Although there were only 32 tons of tank and eight tons of silt, which added up to 40 tons, the effort needed had to be multiplied by 10, because the tank was being dragged through a wall of shingle. The cables kept snapping and there were constant minor snags. But all the time, the engineers kept saying: 'No problem, no problem,' and slowly it kept coming up the beach. Eventually it cleared the beach. It was time for the treatment people I had organised, a firm called Fertan, to take over. The rust treatment experts had told me that they would need to work on it as soon as it came out of the sea, and they organised a firm of high-pressure water cleaners to clean the surface before they treated it. I remember the vans being in the car park where the tank was eventually going to be. On the side of one van was the description, 'Tank Cleaning'. Of course that did not apply to Army tanks but to washing out old petrol tanks under garages which had closed down. It reminded me of my bank manager and his enquiry about the type of water tank I was buying.

It was dark by now, but they worked hard throughout the night blasting off the barnacles and other crustaceans. Next day, the Fertan treatment people painted it with a cosmetic coat of preservative. We were steadily getting closer to raising the tank up on its plinth, but at this point came the one part of the operation I had not planned. How were we to get it over the road? The council had kindly agreed to provide a site, but I still had to move the tank the last few yards onto it. I suddenly thought this was going to mean lifting the tank with a crane, a piece of equipment we simply did not have. I was not even sure that a crane strong enough could be found in Devon. But, when the tank reached the sea wall and it was turned round to point up the concrete ramp, one of the most extraordinary miracles of the whole project took place.

As the tracks touched concrete instead of shingle, they started to turn. There were still metal strops from the flotation bags trapped between the running wheels, and some people there who obviously thought they were military vehicle experts, said we would have to be careful not to snap the tracks, but they were moving. All the tracks were moving. Nor did they suffer any damage from the flotation bag strops. It needed only the towing power of the large bulldozer for the tank to come up the concrete ramp as smoothly as if it had been built the day before, not 40 years previously. The black crustaceans and the mud were falling off the tracks and they were going around quite freely. Towing it across the road turned out to be no problem at all. But on this one occasion we kept winching without a break and the traffic backed up for two or three miles towards Kingsbridge.

The police were in attendance from all over the South Hams, and they had their work cut out. I remember one policeman was supposed to be going home to take his wife out to dinner, but he did not want to leave. He got into trouble at home for that. Indeed, nobody wanted to leave the tank now that we were so close to home. At one stage, after we had had a rather lengthy winching session, and the traffic had built up particularly badly, we decided to lower the cable and let them pass, but no traffic came. All the drivers had got out of their cars from miles back up the road, to stand and watch the tank come to rest.

With the wheels and tracks turning, we towed it with the large bulldozer over the road, down the slope into the car park, and towards its plinth. Much of this part of the journey was downhill. The council had cut out a large area of the wall of the car park to let the tank in. The tracks were now running so smoothly that the tank was starting to catch up with the bulldozer, and we got it into the car park and next to its plinth just in time.

It stayed there overnight with me watching. I did not go to sleep at all that night, I just stood by the tank. After all that effort and all the worry and everything that had gone on, to see that tank next to its plinth was heart-stopping. I just cannot describe the feeling. This was something I believe I had been given to do, and I had finally succeeded.

The next morning, it was all hands on deck to wash out the salt water. An engineer pumped in large quantities of fresh water under high pressure but nothing seemed to be happening. The tank was just sitting there, filling with water. The engineer tried to cut underneath with oxyacetylene cutting equipment, but that would barely cut into the surface of the metal, let alone go through it. Forty years under water, and an oxyacetylene cutter would not go anywhere near that metal. Then all of a sudden there was a massive gush from underneath the rear of the tank, by the engine compartment, and the whole lot came pouring out – fresh water, salt water, mud, silt. It was the hole through which all that silt came out which turned out to be the reason why the tank sank in the first place. Underneath the rear of the engine compartment, a watertight metal plate was missing. It could not possibly have just dropped off during the time the tank was in the sea, because I subsequently found out from a tank expert that it took two men half a morning to take the plate off and replace it. It was fitted with countless specialised bolts, to make it totally watertight.

After the silt came out, our team of cleaners descended again. Again the water pressure hose was turned on, and it was not long before I had a shiny black tank. It looked brand new. Of course, its original colour had been drab green, for camouflage, but now, like my clothes, I wanted it to be black. I thought too that a black tank was a suitable reminder of a sombre occasion. If anybody in the future attempted to deface it with graffiti, I was ready with several gallons of black bitumen paint stored in my garage.

I was quite right about the graffiti. On one occasion, in the middle of the night, it was defaced. I frequently went out at night to look at the tank, and once I found white spray-can slogans all over it. They said, 'Ban the bomb' and all the usual things. This was a travesty – the tank was not put there as a symbol of war, but as a symbol of respect to the many young men who had died. My wife and I and a young woman called Sally, who worked in the guesthouse, went down at midnight and spent until four o'clock in the morning repainting the tank with bitumen paint before daylight came. The graffiti artists lost the publicity they were anxious to seek.

The next, and last, stage was to raise the tank onto its plinth. I had known from the outset that I had to have a site for the tank, and quite early on, I rang up the district council. At the time, the chairman of the district council was Mr Percy Moysey and his secretary was Mr Tim Price. I met them in their offices at Totnes and told them what I wanted to do. It seemed most logical and fitting for the tank to be displayed near the beach, and there was some spare ground near the end of the car park between the beach and Slapton Ley. They were both very co-operative, and made approaches to the Field Studies Council, who owned the land, which the council leased. Permission was given for the tank to be displayed on a plinth in that spot. It would be built up out of soil and simple materials and have a pathway round it. Later, special stones would be added to the site.

The bulldozer was brought alongside to tow it up and a chain was attached. For a few moments, when the bulldozer first took the strain, the bulldozer's tracks skidded, then with one or two jerks the tank rolled forward again, up and onto its plinth. Once in place Jim Parrot put blocks behind the tracks to stop it rolling back, and at the same time welded the tracks in place. We had to be very careful to weld it firmly because it was perfectly capable of moving. There was grease coming out of the nipples on the wheels after all that time under water as the high-pressure water pump had blasted some of the sealant off. The actual rubber bogeys were like new, each with a date and the name of the manufacturer on it – Goodyear on one side and Dayton on the other, and if you took a hammer and hit the rubber, it bounced right off, it was still in such good condition.

The moment when the tank actually came to rest on its plinth was one of the greatest moments in my life. It was lowered with its gun pointing towards the sea, and there it was – my tank. It was not a dream any more, it was a reality.

In a sense I might be said to have finished what I set out to do. I had raised the tank. It turned out to be far from the end. The tank was dedicated in a very moving ceremony held at Slapton village church and the bugler played the last post by its side. But afterwards as the days passed, when I looked at it and spent a lot of my time round it, I knew I had done all this, without help from the Americans. It was, after all, their men that lost their lives; it was they who had forgotten; it was they who did not mention their soldiers' sacrifice on the obelisk they had erected 10 years after they lost these men. I knew my next challenge had to be to try to get from the American Government an official memorial to these men who had died.

10

THE MEMORIAL SERVICE

'I felt I had to complain at the highest level. He said, "You have done that."'

After the recovery of the tank and the dedication service, I received two kind letters from the American authorities. The first was from Charles H Price II, the US ambassador to London. At the time I was thrilled to receive an envelope in the post with the ambassador's seal on it. The letter said:

> I would like to register my personal appreciation and that of the United States for your efforts in establishing a memorial to those American servicemen who lost their lives at Slapton Sands during World War II. In particular, your contribution in recovering the tank from offshore was a most generous gesture, for which you have our deep thanks.
>
> Whilst your memorial commemorates our servicemen's ultimate sacrifice for freedom we also remember the hardship endured by the residents of the area during that difficult time in 1944, and the unselfish support of the local community was manifested then as it is now in solidifying the bonds that bind our great nations.
>
> Please accept my personal gratitude and appreciation of the co-operation that you accomplished to place a Sherman tank at the memorial site.

Next to arrive was a letter from Lieutenant Colonel T A Haase, the assistant army attaché in the Embassy, who was to be the only American actually present at the dedication of the tank. He was a very fine man. His father was over here during the war, so it was particularly poignant for him to attend the ceremony. By a huge coincidence, his father trained at Slapton, although he was not involved in the tragedy, and subsequently went across to Normandy. The letter reads:

> I want to personally thank you and congratulate you for the efforts you undertook in bringing about the erection of a memorial to those Americans who gave their lives on Slapton Sands for the preparation of the Normandy invasion.
>
> As a military man, I was deeply moved by the genuine feelings of appreciation towards the US Military that I sensed both at the ceremony, at the church and at the unveiling of the plaque in front of the tank.
>
> You were the major contributor towards the setting up of this memorial to those Americans and I wish to express on my personal behalf and on behalf of all the United States military forces our sincere appreciation for your generous and unselfish contributions.

I thought when I received those letters that there must be some way to use that sense of gratitude for what I had done to obtain the official recognition for the dead of Exercise Tiger that I was seeking. But I could not at first see where to start. Then, about a year after the tank was raised and set on its plinth, I had a visit from a retired American army major in the 70th US Tank Battalion. His name was Attlee Wampler, and on a visit to Devon he had gone to see my tank. Subsequently he came to see me at my house with his wife Janet, and offered me an invitation to attend the 70th Tank Battalion Assoication reunion, in Harrisburg, Pennsylvania, so that they could thank me for what I had done for their men. This would be an opportunity to take my case over to the United States. I did not know how, but I felt sure that if I could get to the American authorities in person, I could make progress. So I accepted the invitation and went over to America in September 1985. I was treated in a royal manner; I stayed with Attlee and Janet, but I only had one day's rest.

There were a lot of lovely people there, all veterans of the 70th Tank. I picked up snippets of information to add to my collection and stayed at different veterans' homes. I was taken on a tour of New York by a lawyer who was a veteran. I visited Washington and Baltimore and Chesapeake and all around that part of the United States. To show their appreciation for what I had done in raising the tank, they often made me the guest of honour at functions. For one raffle prize, they had a big Afghan. An Afghan in America is a huge bedspread, which is knitted or crocheted in multicolours. I must admit it caught my eye and I bought tickets for it. There were several hundred people there and they all determined that no matter who won, it was going to be mine anyway. I could not lose, and I brought it back home with me.

I also found out a great deal more about Exercise Tiger and about my own tank. The swimming tank, I discovered, was first invented by a Hungarian-born British engineer, called Nicholas Straussler. Basically, it consisted of a collapsible screen built around a water-proofed tank. The screen was fitted in such a way as to create the displacement of water required for a heavy object like a tank to float. Fixed to the collapsible screen were rubber tubes which were inflated using compressed air contained in two bottles mounted on the hull front. The rubberised screen was held in place by a steel frame which also protected the screen from the water pressure outside.

This design was known as the Duplex Drive (or DD) because it could operate both on land and at sea, and the use of the DD in the assault on the Normandy coast in the summer of 1944 was ordered by General Eisenhower as a result of demonstrations he had seen in January of that year.

In the water, the swimming DD was driven by two contra-rotating, 26 inch diameter propellers, and travelled at a speed of about 5 knots. The propellers were pivoted to port or starboard either hydraulically by the driver inside, or manually by the commander in order to steer the DD. The commander had a small platform welded to the starboard rear of the turret and was provided with a detachable tiller and basic navigational equipment. When the screen was raised, the tank's height was increased from nine to 13 feet. The Duplex Drive tanks were known to be unstable in other than very calm conditions. Before launching, they raised the flotation collar with hydraulics and on reaching land they lowered the flotation collar and there was a fighting tank. But they were probably more suited to crossing a river than being out in the open sea, because the whole of the tank itself was suspended beneath the water, the flotation collar being above it.

Tactically speaking, the DD tank did have its advantages. It presented a small target when at sea; it would surprise the enemy as it came ashore, dropped its screen and engaged them in a matter of seconds. It could also reduce risks to the safety of the LCT as they could stand well off the beaches during the initial action resulting from the first assault.

To the crew of the vehicle, however, the story was completely different. They, apart from the commander if he was outside and the driver who possibly had a periscope extension, could neither see nor hear anything outside. What they did know was that with the top of their tank below sea level, there would be very little chance of escape if the flotation equipment were to be damaged, causing the vehicle to be swamped and to sink like a stone. They had only their periscopes and instruments to enable them to see where they were going, and the flotation collar was so high that they could not possibly fire the main gun with it up.

The commander of my tank was Orris Johnson. In Harrisburg, he explained to me how he thought the tank had come to sink. It was in the earlier part of Exercise Tiger. There were two tanks on the LST, and the one I had recovered was in the rear. When the tank in front raised its flotation collar to launch, instead of engaging forward gear it engaged reverse, causing it to collide with the front of the other. It then launched successfully. Orris, the commander of the second tank, got out and inspected it for any damage, but he could not see any. However, when he launched it only went ahead about 15 feet before it sank. All the crew got out safely and climbed back aboard the landing craft. Until my meeting with him in Harrisburg, he always put the blame on a split in the flotation screen which he had not noticed. I told him that when the tank was recovered, we had discovered that there was a watertight metal plate missing underneath the engine compartment. It was a very large plate, which I subsequently found out took two men nearly half a day to take off and replace. It was fitted with numerous watertight bolts, because any water in the engine would have disabled it. So I was able to tell the tank's commander what he had not known for 40 years. When the tank, with its nine cylinder petrol driven aircraft engine at full revs, launched in the sea with that plate missing, the water would gush in and the steam from it would be immense. Of course that was precisely what had happened.

It had always been rumoured that another tank had sunk at about the same time, causing the loss of two lives. But it remained just a rumour for many years until one day I received a phone call and subsequently a letter from an English naval diver who was stationed at Dartmouth at the time. He had been called to Slapton Sands and taken over a bridge that had been built across the lake to the other side. There he was taken to a tented headquarters, sworn to secrecy by American officers, and told that he had to go and look for a tank that had sunk about 100 yards offshore.

They had lost this tank on the dummy run into the shore and two men had lost their lives in it. They brought a recovery vessel from Plymouth and the equipment to recover it, as it was so close inshore. They said the hatch would probably be open and they wanted him to get inside and put the tank into neutral. Now this was rather difficult. He was a diver and did not know how to put a tank in neutral. Furthermore, there would be no chance of his getting inside a tank in the diving gear he was wearing, the old-fashioned helmet and heavy boot type. All the same, he went down to the seabed and walked around. He could speak to the surface from that particular type of suit, and he called up to say all he could see was a sheet of white canvas. He did not realise it at the time, but this was, of course, the flotation screen, still in place. They said that was what he was looking for and he had to get inside. The hatch was open, but knowing that they had lost two men on it, he simply could not bring himself to go inside. So he just put his left foot inside and wiggled it around. He could not feel anything soft, and that was as far as he was prepared to go. He attached a buoy to the tank to guide the lifting crew and then came up. As the tank was being recovered he was on his way back to his post in Dartmouth and he never knew any more about it.

After I had attended the reunion, I was given a plaque by

the 70th US Tank Battalion Association and also became an honorary member. I found the reunion a very moving experience, and it is wonderful to have the plaque to remind me of those days. It states:

> The 70th Tank Battalion Association takes great pleasure in presenting this Certificate of Appreciation to Mr Kenneth Small. Whereas Kenneth has expended much time, effort and personal finance re the salvaging of a Duplex Drive Amphibious Tank of the Battalion from the depths of the English Channel and has now mounted and dedicated this tank as a memorial to the American Servicemen who made the supreme sacrifice during training exercises in the area of Devon, England.
>
> Therefore let it be known to all that the 70th Tank Battalion presents this certificate to Mr Small as a token of our esteem and appreciation for his efforts in honoring our comrades.

But while finding out more about the tank was fascinating, it was not helping me in my quest for official recognition of the dead in Exercise Tiger. However, to my great satisfaction, the trip to the States helped me in that direction as well. The day after the reunion, a young American arrived at the house. His name was Doug Mathias, and he informed me that he and Attlee were going to take me to meet a congresswoman in the Capitol building in Washington DC, some two to three hours drive away. This could be where I might have the opportunity of trying to persuade the administration to assist me in the memorial I was determined to get.

We went to the Capitol building and I was shown around, and then summoned to her office. Her name was Congresswoman Beverly Byron and she was the representative for Maryland, and also a very powerful member of the US Armed Services Committee. I remember the first thing Congresswoman Byron did when I went into her office and shook hands with her was to come up and look closely at the jewel around my neck which is made up of jewellery found on the beach. I told her about it and then sat down and put my case to her, requesting her support for an official memorial. The meeting went on for about an hour. At the end of that time she opened her desk, and produced a book, which none of her staff had seen before. She opened the book and showed me that it was written by her father, Captain Harry Butcher, in 1946 – two years after the tragedy. The book was called *My Three Years with Ike* and it covered the time when Harry Butcher was Eisenhower's aide. He was actually over here during the planning of the exercise and witnessed the sinking of the tank. His was the criticism of many of the men as 'green as corn'. In fact, the only fault in his description of the sinking of the tank was the fact that he talked of seeing smoke coming from the tank and the men then clambering back on board the landing craft. As subsequent events turned out, this was not smoke but steam, because the plate underneath the engine had been left off, as we discovered when we took it ashore. When the tank hit the water, the cold water on the very powerful aircraft engine in the tank obviously created great clouds of steam.

Beverly Byron said that she would give me her full support, which of course pleased me greatly. The very next day she made a speech in Congress, thanking me in a very personal way for what I had done as regards the tank. It was 11 September 1985.

> Mr Speaker, today I would like to pay tribute to 749 American soldiers who lost their lives during Exercise Tiger, a secret preparatory operation for the Normandy invasion during World War II. During this operation, the US 4th Infantry division losses were numbered at approximately 749 men, and many more were wounded. The Allied military command did little to recognise those individuals who participated. Few people have heard of this tragedy some 41 years later. Mr Speaker, a memorial was recently erected to honor those men who lost their lives in the line of duty. The memorial, which stands in Torcross, was not established by a military authority, but by a distinguished gentleman from England. Yesterday I had the privilege of meeting this gentleman. Mr Ken Small of Torcross in Devon County, England, pursued, at his own expense, the idea of

> establishing a memorial for over 10 years. On 9 November 1984, Mr Small's dream became a reality. On that day his memorial to those who served in the operation was dedicated. I, personally, am proud of Mr Small's actions and hope others will recognise his efforts to pay tribute to those who served in Operation Tiger, those fallen soliders.

Following on from that speech, she successfully had a bill passed in Congress authorising the funds for a special plaque to be provided for the memorial service. But that was to take some time. Meanwhile, I came back to England. By this time I was becoming known through press coverage, and I started to meet more and more survivors. After the memorial service the letters started flowing in from America by the hundred, from relatives, survivors and well-wishers. I became a focal point for a lot of survivors' letters.

I was also in contact with the authorities in the Pentagon, with a view to acquiring all the official records of the exercise. They were forthcoming in huge piles. I acquired a list of the dead, action reports of all the craft, burial reports and injury reports. I doubt that there is anything of significance about the exercise that the Americans have kept from me, although a lot of the relatives had difficulty in finding it all out.

Indeed, one reason why what I did here was so appreciated in America was that the relatives had tried for so many years to find out more about their lost loved ones, how they died, where they died and where they were buried, and all they had met with was red tape and brick walls. I found out in the later stages of my campaign that it does not pay to try and attempt to write any request to America. Ninety-nine per cent of anything I did in this whole project was done on the telephone, expensive though it might be. I found that was the only way to reach the people with whom I wanted to speak. If you write, and the relatives probably did, the letter finishes up at some minor office, and then somebody usually digs up a regulation which forbids or stone-walls any request.

I had one particular example of that myself, much later. I thought I would like comments from the secretary of defence, secretary of Army and secretary of Navy for this book, as a foreword. This time I thought I would include these requests in a letter, thanking them at the same time for their past co-operation. All I got back were letters from minor officials stating that it was not Government policy for senior members of the administration to do such things, and as many requests were received they had to say no. This was disappointing, so I rang up one of my contacts, and told her of this letter and she asked me who had signed it. When I told her, she replied that the man obviously did not realise what I had done, and I should leave it with her. I got my letter. The reason I quote that incident is because that is what happened to so many people when they tried to get information. Instead of trying to go to the top, they tried to work through the system in the accepted manner of writing. But these departments in America are vast, and it is very easy for a letter to get lost in the Pentagon or the Capitol.

Another thing that happened in the period after the dedication was an incident that brought the war quite close to home. We had a house full of guests one July, and early one evening I had a phone call from another guesthouse proprietor in the village to say that a bomb had been washed up under my sea wall. Our sea wall is only about 10 yards from the front of our house and from the dining room where all the guests were. I thought he was pulling my leg, But he was serious. Two divers had just come to his house to say they were diving off our beach and found a bomb which they brought ashore and left under our wall. I went down onto the beach, and it was there, a thing about two feet long and six inches wide, pointed at one end and blunt at the other. I could see the channel where they had dragged it through the shingle from the water and left it under the wall. The cover was off and a creamy white liquid was oozing out. I wasted no time. I called the police and the coastguard, and the bomb disposal people immediately came round.

The bomb disposal officer from Plymouth looked at it and said he was not moving it. If the sun got on it the following day, it would blow up. He would have to blow it up where it was. Not right there, surely, I asked. He said he would take it well beyond our wall back to the cliff above our beach and

THE WHITE HOUSE

WASHINGTON

April 12, 1988

Dear Mr. Small:

On behalf of all Americans, thank you for your kind and generous efforts in helping to establish a memorial at Torcross, England, honoring the brave American soldiers and sailors who died in 1944 during a rehearsal for the D-Day landings of World War II.

Your concern for our servicemen who made the supreme sacrifice exemplifies the strong bonds of friendship and admiration that unite the people of our two countries. This memorial has strengthened those bonds by reminding us of the untold sacrifices and contributions of citizens such as yourself who endured countless hardships for a common cause.

The tragic loss of lives in April 1944 vividly reminds us that freedom is not free, but requires the steadfast courage and dedication of men and women who are willing to fight to safeguard that freedom.

Soldiers of the NATO Alliance today, like those in 1944, stand ready to defend freedom, and your compassion serves as an inspiration not only to them but to all those who cherish freedom throughout the world. God bless you.

Sincerely,

Ronald Reagan

Mr. Kenneth Small
The Cove Guest House
Torcross
Kingbridge
South Devon TQ7 2TH
England

The letter I was proud to receive – from the US President to a Devon hotelier

The flotation tanks were put round the tank and slowly, after almost 40 years on the sea bed, the tank rose to the surface.

The tank slowly approached the shore.

A proud moment indeed, the tank was finally on dry land.

The tank needed careful cleaning and oiling, work even went on at night (above).

100TH CONGRESS
1ST SESSION

H. R. 314

To authorize the Secretary of Defense to prepare a plaque honoring American servicemen who lost their lives during "Operation Tiger" in April 1944.

IN THE HOUSE OF REPRESENTATIVES

JANUARY 6, 1987

Mrs. BYRON introduced the following bill; which was referred to the Committee on Armed Services

---

A BILL

To authorize the Secretary of Defense to prepare a plaque honoring American servicemen who lost their lives during "Operation Tiger" in April 1944.

Be it enacted by the Senate and House of Representatives of the United States of America in Congress assembled, That the Secretary of Defense shall prepare a plaque honoring all American servicemen who lost their lives at Slapton Sands, Torcross, England, between April 26 and April 28, 1944, during "Operation Tiger", a secret exercise which served as a rehearsal for the invasion of Normandy, and shall make arrangements for the placement of such plaque at the Operation Tiger Memorial in Torcross.

○

The Bill put through the House of Representatives thanks to Beverley Byron, allowing the memorial to be erected.

THE SECRETARY OF THE NAVY

WASHINGTON, D.C. 20350-1000

15 August 1988

Mr. Kenneth Small
The Cove Guest House
Torcross Kingsbridge
South Devon TQ7 2TH
England

Dear Mr. Small,

Please accept the U.S. Navy's sincere appreciation for your time and effort in establishing the memorial at Slapton Sands to honor the servicemen who were lost in the World War II Operation TIGER.

Without your strong support and enthusiasm, the commemoration would not have been possible.

I wish you continued success with your forthcoming projects.

Sincerely,

William L. Ball, III

I was delighted to meet Beverley Byron (left) who put the Bill through the House of Representatives. I was also privileged to meet William Taft (top right) and to receive a letter from William Ball, Secretary to the Navy (top). However, the most moving have been the tributes from the relatives of those who died, for example this heartfelt acknowledgement (bottom right).

The Men and Families of
The 3891st QM Truck Company
U. S. Army
Present This

Certificate of Appreciation

to

Ken Small

For His Devotion to Honoring the Casualties and the Survivors of Operation Tiger, the Tragedy of April 27, 1944 at Slapton Sands, Devon, England, that Will Forever Let the World Know What Happened There. We Acknowledge our Thanks and our Deepest Feelings.

Manly Aylor, Capt.

At last the tank and plaque – after more than 40 years a fitting memorial to young men who unnecessarily lost their lives.

blow it up there. Then he said he would need some help. The policeman said that he would look after matters at the guesthouse, and the coastguard immediately decided he had got another appointment. That left me to go and help the bomb disposal officer.

Bomb disposal officers have to be fearless, I suppose, but I am not. We went down to the bomb and he said we would make a small wooden stretcher to carry it beyond the sea wall and back onto the cliff. There he would blow it up. Then he started scraping at it with a penknife. I asked what he was doing, and he said he was seeing if it was a dud. I wondered how he would know. Without a trace of a smile, he replied that it would have 'dud' written on it. Very dry he was. Anyway, we made a stretcher and carried it to the far end of the beach and back onto the cliff. By this time it was dark, and I went across with a torch and shone the light while he put a small amount of plastic explosive on the bomb. I remember there was a snail in the undergrowth. He picked it up and put it on the bomb, and said, 'Mate you are in for a hell of a shock.' Then he started measuring the fuse wire, to blow it. He was just putting two fingers apart, saying, '10 seconds, 20 seconds'. I thought to myself that he might have been a bit more accurate about this. But he measured out about 25 seconds of fuse wire. It was not the old-fashioned sort, this wire is connected to the explosive and has a ring at the end of it. The idea is that you pull the ring, which sets off the fuse and then you run. He told me I could pull the ring, then we would have 25 seconds to get to cover. We had already chosen the rock in front of the house behind which we should crouch.

When I pulled the ring it was like a penny firecracker going off; it scared the hell out of me. Then I ran with him to the rock. He said I should put my head well down between my arms and keep it well tucked in. I wondered if it really was going to make that much of a bang. It did. When it went off, it blew a great hole in the side of the cliff and for several seconds afterwards we could hear shrapnel dropping in the sea. The whole house was covered in a black dust because the cove is made mainly of slate. Then there were phone calls from villagers wanting to know what was going on, and the coastguard reappeared along with the policeman. The bomb disposal officer and I were talking about it when the two divers who had found it in the first place came back. They more or less said weren't they good for finding that thing out there and bringing it ashore. You can imagine what reply they got from all of us.

There was the question of where all the money for the project was to come from. I had no other means of income than the guesthouse and the campaign was taking me deeper and deeper into debt. But I was committed to it. I believe I was chosen to do this and I just kept on paying out. At no point did I ever think of giving up, and if the cost had been double what it was, I would still have carried on. Some time in the future, I hoped things would straighten themselves out.

The business we own here is all ours. The property is now worth quite a lot of money, but that is the only collateral that we have. There was never any difficulty in getting money from the bank as long as it was on the security of the property. As for the day to day upkeep of the tank, I had a meeting with the treatment firm, Fertan, who had treated it in the first instance and they agreed they would carry on treating it. When it began to look a bit untidy after the winter storms I would ring them up and they would send down a man or two to smarten it up. I have that done now at least once a year, and they very kindly make no charge. I think the product they use speaks for itself. When you look at that tank now and think it has been up four and a half years and spent 40 years on the seabed, and yet you can hit it anywhere with a hammer and strike solid metal, you could not ask for a better testimonial for any preservative.

Impatient as I am, I kept ringing up to see how things were going in the United States. I phoned Beverly Byron's co-ordinator Doug Mathias and his wife many many times, pushing and pushing. Of course I realised these people were busy, but I felt that I had to keep pushing on. One day the idea came to me to try ringing the then US defence secretary,

Caspar Weinberger. I telephoned him at his office in Washington and was connected with a lady called Melba Bowling who was the secretary to William Taft, the deputy to Mr Weinberger. I asked if I could speak with Mr Weinberger or Mr Taft or meet with them. She said they were very busy men, so I decided that I would tell her my whole story. After all I was speaking to the very heart of the administration. When I had explained what I wanted and why, I left it at that. Just two days later Melba Bowling telephoned me to say that Mr Taft would meet with me in his office at the Pentagon at 10.00 am on 16 May 1987.

I could hardly believe what I was hearing, but it was true. The trip was hastily organised and off I went to America again. Once again, I was taken in tow by Doug Mathias, and he was every bit as thrilled as I was. We were to visit the Pentagon, and he had never been in there either, although he had been serving Beverly Byron for seven years. The experience of going into that building, into literally the bowels of the earth, to meet with the deputy US defence secretary, was quite daunting. First of all after much security searching we arrived at a door with what looked like two model soldiers guarding it. They just did not look real, those Marines. They did not move an inch, not a centimetre, not even a millimetre, and they were so smart. We went into the outer office, and there was as I recall a young uniformed and very attractive woman who sat us down in some extremely plush furniture and gave us coffee in white bone china cups with gold round the rim and the Pentagon crest. We were there for about 15 minutes and then Melba Bowling came through and took us into her office, and said that Mr Taft would be through in a moment. He was with Mr Weinberger signing documents just in the very next office.

Mr Taft's office was extremely impressive. I recall the beautiful pictures on the wall, the furniture and the bookcases. But what sticks in my mind to this day is that on his desk was an enormous book headed *The Soviet War Machine*. Bearing in mind that this was the time of the missile crisis , people had told me that I would be lucky if I got five minutes with Mr Taft. I however wanted his support for the official memorial. I realised the whole thing was not going to be easy; I had Beverly Byron's support, but the more support I got the more I thought I was likely to succeed. Mr Taft asked me about my life, and how I came to do what I had done and was totally supportive of my aims to get these men properly recognised. In fact, I spent nearly an hour and an quarter with him and his military assistant, Colonel Goodbary, and it was I who ran out of things to ask him in relation to the support I needed and not he who ushered me out after a brief meeting. He instructed Colonel Goodbary to get in touch with the secretary of the Army's office and to start the whole ball rolling – which is exactly what they did.

After I had seen Mr Taft, I came back to England. But then the bureaucratic wheels seemed to grind very slowly. It was like the tank really I suppose. I wanted them to turn from being stuck to going round fast. So, over the next months, I spent many hours on the phone to the Pentagon, on the phone to Beverly Byron's officials and on the phone to countless colonels. I cannot name them all but there were at least 15 different colonels, and colonels in America are very powerful people. They are capable of making big decisions. This always puzzled me when making comparisons between England and America; a colonel in the English Army is a high ranking officer, but there are many more above him. The thing that stuck in my mind was Colonel Oliver North and the problem of the Irangate scandal. When I watched it on the news I wondered how a colonel could have so much influence. But I soon found out why.

I remember the colonel who said to me, 'Man, you have three mountains of bureaucracy to climb. You went up the first and down it. You went up the second and down it. Now you are halfway up the third. How the hell you have done it I don't know, but I will give you my support fully.' That is what went on through the whole system; I never received one single word of discouragement from any official in the US Government or their departments. Having met with Melba Bowling, the deputy defence secretary's secretary, my next contact was Barbara Freudberg in the secretary of the Army's office and subsequent to that Miss Judy Vanbenthuysen, in the secretary for the Navy's office. These women had a very major part to play in my success, there was no doubt.

By now I was making progress. After I had been to see Beverly Byron the first time, she made her speech. Then, after I had been to see Mr Taft, the next stage was the official bill, the original of which I was sent by Beverly Byron, thanking me for all my efforts. It is among my most prized possessions. After all, how many Englishmen can say that they had a bill put through the American Congress? It was Bill HR314 in the House of Representatives, 6 January 1987.

> A Bill to authorise the Secretary of Defense to prepare a plaque honoring the American servicemen who lost their lives during Operation Tiger in April 1944. Be it enacted between the Senate and the House of Representatives of the United States of America and Congress assembled, that the Secretary of Defense shall prepare a plaque for all the American servicemen who lost their lives at Slapton Sands, Torcross, England, between April 26th and April 28th 1944 during Operation Tiger, a secret exercise which served as a rehearsal for the invasion of Normandy and shall make arrangements for the placement of such plaque at the Operation Tiger memorial in Torcross.

But even though the funds were authorised, there was a long way between actually getting the money and holding the ceremony. The whole affair became more and more complex because the secretary for the Army had passed on the responsibility of organising the military attendance to the base at Heidelberg in Germany. It was from there that a party would set out including an American three-star general, the general commanding the US Seventh Corps in Europe, and also a full honour guard, all of whom would be flown in specially to attend the ceremony. It was also agreed that a party of officials were to come from Washington. This would include Beverly Byron, General Mark Clark's son, and a man called Charles McDonald, a historian whom the Pentagon had appointed to come and answer questions to the press about this particular exercise. That was the official party.

This was all happening in the United States. In the meantime, I was trying to make contacts with the UK authorities. Obviously, this meant talking to the local council. When the idea first came up, one council official had suggested that we should think in terms of inviting somebody really important: if not the queen, then one of the royal dukes or perhaps Mrs Thatcher. The dukes in particular could be said to have a connection. They all had associations with the Royal Naval College at Dartmouth. The Britannia Royal Naval College served as a hospital for the men who were wounded in Exercise Tiger. Indeed those who were in Dartmouth at the time remember it was possible to walk across the river in the dark literally without touching water, so great were the numbers of US ships in the river.

But when it came nearer the day, the chief executive of the council seemed to play the idea down by saying that the security problems of inviting such important personages would be immense for the council. I could not really express an opinion about that, I know the security people have their problems. But it was a nice thought by the official who proposed it and obviously it would have been nice if somebody of that calibre had attended the ceremony. The council invited several other people to the memorial service. They invited the defence minster, Mr Younger, they invited the Lord Lieutenant of Devon, they invited our own MP, Mr Anthony Steen, and they invited the flag officer, Plymouth.

I had already had some differences with the council over the ceremony in that they had informed me that they wanted only a low-key religious content. I did not approve of this. In fact, the religious content of the memorial service as it turned out was far far less than the one for the dedication of the tank. But it was council opinion that the tank dedication service in the church had 'gone on, and had rambled on a bit' as one council member put it.

That was Mr Percy Moysey who was the chairman at the time the tank was recovered. On this and several other items I disagreed with the council, and at a very heated meeting between council officials and myself I put as I recall five objections to their plans. On each objection, I was squashed by the council. As each one was dismissed, I was getting madder and madder. Eventually I stormed out of the meeting, saying that I would not attend the ceremony under these circumstances.

The secretary came out and begged me to go back, but I would not. For a long time I did not want to go. I said I would not attend the memorial service, rather than succumb to having all these matters dismissed, which I thought were very reasonable requests. In the end, I came round, but then there was a shock when the replies to the invitations came in. The council told me that they had invited quite a list of people and that among others they had invited the defence minister. In addition, they had requested that in the event of his not being able to attend, would he appoint somebody in his place. The reply was that the defence minster could not attend, but no mention was made of appointing anyone in his place. The Lord Lieutenant had replied to the effect that he had another appointment, the flag officer, Plymouth, had another appointment, his deputy had another appointment, and our local MP had another appointment.

It is worth bearing in mind that these other appointments did not only apply to the memorial service, they applied to two events. The district council had also organised an official reception for the American delegation at the Britannia Royal Naval College on the Saturday evening, where they were to have a dinner to welcome them. The other invitation of course was to the ceremony itself the following day at 12:30 pm on Sunday, 15 November. They had turned down two invitations, all of them, and this infuriated me. I was really livid, because I could not believe that all these people had suddenly acquired other appointments. I appreciated the council point of view, that they could do little about it, but I felt I should and ought to act, so yet again I got on the phone. First of all I thought I would get in touch with the prime minister. I went through about three phone calls to different secretaries in Downing Street, until eventually a man who seemed to be in some sort of authority answered the phone. I had to repeat my story to each of these people and gradually I was getting higher and higher up the ladder. I told this man my story and said I just felt I had to complain at the highest possible level. He said to me: 'Well you have certainly done that.'

I had got pretty close to the prime minister. He said of course I had to realise, bearing in mind I was complaining about the lack of attendance of the defence minister at that time, that his job was concerned with the movements of the prime minister and not her ministers. Nonetheless, he said he would look into it. I put the phone down, and my next thought was that I would ring the office of Mr Steen, our MP, in the House of Commons. I spoke with his secretary and she was quite pert and said he needed months and months of notice for such things. I did not accept that for one moment and I thought at some future date I would write for his official reasons for not attending. I did so, and his letter of reply left me even more disgusted than before. It seemed to me that he was acting like a spoilt child when he said that he did not want to be involved in the 'general melée' of things, to use his words.

Then I thought I would try ringing the defence minister, and yet again had to go through two or three secretaries. Then eventually a man answered the phone and said, 'Martin Helm speaking.' I thought: Martin Helm, I know that name. Then my mind clicked back to the refusal of Army help when I was winching the tank ashore. It was Helm and Major Gugdeon who had stopped the help. I did not mention this at first. Helm said that the defence minister was a very busy man and his attitude was quite 'who do you think you are?' on the phone. Then, as I went through the story with him, I said: 'Oh, by the way do I know you? Did you work with Major Gudgeon?' He said: 'Yes, but what's that got to do with you?' I replied, 'It was you and he who put a stop to the Army's helping me to recover this tank as a memorial in the first place.' Then I put the phone down on him, as they had done to me all those years past.

Three-quarters of an hour later, he phoned me back a completely different man, courteous and polite, saying that he had arranged for a brigadier from Exeter to attend the memorial service on behalf of the defence minister. They could hardly have found one much closer, Exeter only being an hour's drive away from Torcross. Then the Lord Lieutenant arranged for General Sir Peter Whiteley to represent him. I contacted the flag officer, Plymouth, and objected to his non-attendance and his deputy's. But I just got a very official letter saying that on these occasions it was normal for responsibility to be passed down to the commander of the Britannia Royal Naval College. I could not argue with that. But I still think that the whole British attendance was pathetic. It could not have been possible that all these people had other appointments.

I have thought about this a great deal since then and I honestly cannot say why the British were so unenthusiastic. After all there was a very major British involvement in this exercise; there were 32 British vessels involved in it, ranging down from heavy cruisers, through destroyers and corvettes to mine sweepers. Then there were English naval personnel acting as beach masters on the beach. They used to march all the way from Dartmouth to Slapton every day to assist the Americans. There were Navy divers, one of whom recovered the second tank, that was sunk much closer inshore. Perhaps the flag officer, Plymouth, did not know his history well and was unaware of the involvement of Plymouth in the exercise. After all it was Plymouth where HMS *Scimitar* put in when she was holed. Unless, of course, the Royal Navy was embarrassed to be reminded of what was one of their less glorious nights. But the Americans had no such qualms and they had suffered the greatest casualties.

Something else that was a disappointment was the attitude of the local council. At the time of the dedication, it did not seem that the council were being very helpful and by the time we were approaching the memorial service the council and I were clearly at loggerheads. I suppose the seeds were sown when that council official mentioned to me that it was the sort of occasion that should be attended by a member of the royal family. I suppose in that respect I obviously agreed, thinking in terms of Prince Charles or Prince Andrew, and then when the council downgraded it for reasons, as they put it, of security, that was a disappointment. Obviously we did have our differences of opinion. But having said that I would give them credit for the fact that they did do justice to the memorial service by organising a much improved plinth for the ceremony, cobblestoned all round, and they put down a new path.

The strange thing about it, though, is that after the tank was dedicated, in the period before the memorial service, the site itself was sadly neglected. No council officials ever appeared to remove weeds or anything. The paths that were laid around it were covered to the point where you could not see them. I had rung up many times to see if a workman could spend half an hour or even an hour a month, with weedkiller, but I never got any response at all from them. Then in the middle of all this I had a letter from the council – from their legal department – requesting that I lease the tank to the council for periods of 10 years, for nothing. They would maintain the site and I would maintain the tank. This was a little bit more than I could take, so I ignored the letter for two or three months. Back came a reminder, an inevitable reminder, I suppose. I ignored that, and another one. Eventually they sent me a letter ending with the fact that they could ask me to move the tank within a certain period of time.

That really made me mad. By this time, I was ready to put pen to paper and I wrote a very long letter to the council explaining the reasons why the thing was there in the first place, and what I had done, and also that I would have the tank removed by the end of the following month at my own expense. The attitude of the council changed radically from that point on, because the tank had become so well known throughout the whole area. It had become a major tourist feature to countless people from all over England and indeed all over the world. So the idea of leasing was dropped. I was not prepared to pass a sort of semi-ownership over to the council, because while I had ownership of it, I felt that at least I had some say in what should happen to it and what was around it.

The memorial service eventually came together – mainly through my involvement with the secretary for the Army's office, after having met the defence secretary, and subsequently with the unit in Heidelberg. I recall one instance when things were going pretty slowly, and I rang up my contact in the secretary of the Army's office. She went in to try and gee things up a bit. She told me that her boss had said to her that she had better send a signal off to Heidelberg and – she is a wonderful lady – her response to that was, 'No sir, I think you better had.' Anyway, things did pick up and the date was fixed for Sunday, 15 November 1987.

The site now had a lot of improvements made to it. Workmen moved in and put in more boulders, put down more pathways, and relaid part of the plinth around the tank. They hand-set cobblestones into the ground and they put black posts near the car park to stop any cars going right up to the tank. In addition to that the tank dedication plaque, which was put originally on a block of concrete, was remounted. It was surfaced with about half an inch of marble or granite. The district council had invited me to choose the granite on which the memorial plaque was to be mounted from a quarry in Cornwall. Although I know that places in Cornwall had some involvement in Tiger as well, it really took place in Devon, and I thought it more appropriate to get Devon granite. So they took me to Merryvale Quarry on Dartmoor to select the boulder. When we came back I thought it would be nice if a slightly smaller boulder of similar shape could be included instead of the semi-artificial one with the tank plaque on it. Then they would blend together. This was agreed, so I went back and picked a smaller one for the tank memorial, and the plaque was removed from its original base and put onto the new one that I had chosen.

When the plaque was very nearly complete, I received a letter from a man called William Kuntz. He was on the American Navy side of the exercise and he pointed out to me that the Navy side of the exercise had not been mentioned on the suggested inscription. They had in fact lost about 183 men. This disturbed me. His letter was very moving and requested my help on this particular point. I immediately rang the Pentagon and told them, but they said it was too late because the plaque was very nearly complete and ready for shipment. I said it had got to be put right if at all possible. A few days later they rang me up to say that it would be put on:

the Navy side would be mentioned. When I contacted Mr Kuntz by telephone all I can say is, he was in tears. He said on the phone, 'Thanks a million, you have made my day.'

The evening before the ceremony was very grand. I was invited to have dinner after a reception at the Dart Marina Hotel in Dartmouth with my wife and the whole American delegation and the council officials. That was an experience that I will never forget, because not only was it an honour to move through the portals of the Britannia Royal Naval College, escorted as each person was by one of the cadets to the grand dining hall, but the food was immaculate as was the ceremony. Everybody I had met in the United States was there and everybody was enjoying themselves. Sadly the council would not permit anybody to take photographs of the actual dinner, which I thought was a shame. That was another decision of theirs that I disagreed with. After the dinner everybody passed round menus for each person to sign. Altogether it was a very very memorable occasion. During the meal, an American general by the name of Watts came up to me and took a medal out of his pocket and gave it to me. It says 'For distinguished service, given by the Commander of the US Seventh Corps.' He said, 'Mr Small, I give this to my troops who have distinguished themselves; you have distinguished yourself in a most unusual way, would you please accept this medal.' That was truly an honour, and of course I have still got that medal framed on the wall of the guesthouse.

On the Saturday, Beverly Byron and her husband, two friends and her military escort came round to our house to meet the family. In our dining room she presented me with an American Stars and Stripes flag with an official certificate to say that it had been flown from the Capitol building, and thanked me for what I had done. I showed her some of the memorabilia of the tank, in which she was very interested and she spent quite a while here. Then they went for a tour around the South Hams.

The following day, which was Sunday, was the day of the ceremony. Unfortunately it was drizzly, but the council had erected a sort of marquee over the site to protect it from the rain. It was a sombre day and a sombre occasion. The Kingsbridge silver band played some very moving hymns, there was a speech by Beverly Byron then a speech by General Watts, the three star general commanding the US Seventh Corps. The honour guard was standing to attention, and then right at the end of the ceremony, as if nobody had expected it, some 50 or 60 yards away, on a mound, stood a lone American bugler. He played taps, which is the American equivalent of the last post. When that sound drifted down upon the site, I think it would have been difficult to find anybody of the hundreds that were there who did not shed a tear.

After the ceremony, I was taken onto the beach with the honour guard and was photographed and filmed with them on Slapton Sands. From there we went to the Field Centre at Slapton where the warden Mr Shell had organised a buffet for all the dignitaries attending the ceremony. I sat next to Lesley Thomas, the author, and he was extremely impressed with what I had done. But although there was a long line of dignitaries, we were at a fairly casual table. There was a long table where all the council officials sat together with General Sir Peter Whiteley and the commander of the Britannia Royal Naval College. Beverly Byron of course was there and the American delegation and all the other people whom I had met. But at the end of the meal all the British people, the general, and other dignataries just filed out. I never met them and I was never introduced to them which seemed a pity after all my efforts.

11

RELATIVES AND FRIENDS

'At this time, kindly extinguish all smoking materials.'

It was June 1988, and I was aboard flight TW 703 on the final approach to Kansas City airport in the United States. I was due to address several hundred US Army and Navy veterans of World War II at a meeting to commemorate what they had described to me as one of the most costly military exercises of the whole war.

Perhaps I should start by mentioning Evelyn Brannock. She was the instigator of the whole Kansas City meeting. She lost her brother, James Cottrell in the Exercise; he was in one of the Quartermaster Divisions and she had been – like so many in America – obsessed with the search for the truth as to what happened to her relative. She had written to me many times and her letters had been lengthy and sorrowful and very appreciative of what I had done to try and find out exactly what happened during Tiger. Then she decided she would make the trip to England with her family. They came over and visited Madingley Hill Cemetery, Cambridge, where her brother's name was listed on the Wall of the Missing. They were very impressed with the cemetery, and put flowers there. Then they travelled down to see me at Torcross.

The whole family presented me with a plaque with Evelyn's brother's photograph on it in appreciation of what I had done to bring respect and honour to him and the many others. Then we went down to the Tank Memorial where Evelyn laid a wreath of fresh flowers and each member of the family, seven of them altogether, walked down individually to the sea and threw a wreath of roses onto the water. It was then that Evelyn asked me if I would possibly consider coming to attend a meeting she was hoping to have in Kansas on 16 June. I thought about it and I said: 'Look there is no way I can afford the time or the money.'

But she was extremely insistent. Even when my son was taking the family back to the railway station, she said to him, 'You have got to talk about it to your father.' When she got back to America she telephoned me and asked me again to go to Kansas. Something inside me told me I really should go. I made the decision, I booked a flight to Kansas and told Evelyn that I was coming. I could never have imagined what it would be like.

The reception was tears, tears and tears. Evelyn and a number of her friends and their families met me at the airport and they were crying their eyes out: it was about 10 or 15 minutes before I could even get in the car.

They took me to their home in Perry, Kansas and they treated me almost like some super being in gratitude for what I had done. I stayed in Kansas for six days and the meeting – which I had supposed was to be a sort of family gathering – turned out to be a major event. They had had to hire the local American Legion Hall, which is a large building, and there were over 200 people there. Several were survivors from the Exercise, many were relatives of those who had been killed, even mothers and fathers of those who had died. The sad fact is that we do not meet so many of those last now, because they are very old; but that day they made the effort to attend.

We were east of Kansas and the temperatures were hovering around the 110 mark, which was completely foreign to me. Most people would normally keep themselves to themselves, and you saw few of them out in the streets. They were all in their air-conditioned homes trying to avoid the fierce heat. The corn crop was failing and it was quite terrifying that the heat just would not let up.

Evelyn Brannock is a wonderful lady. She has been dedicated like so many others for all these years to finding out about her brother, and she formed a very close bond with me. Another of her brothers, Don, owns some 83 acres of woodland and fishponds in the area and he told me if I came to live out in Kansas there would be a detached house for me and a motor car as well. Her husband Ron works for a truck company. He really is what in Kansas they would call 'a great guy' and a lot of credit is due to him as he has more or less had to take a back seat while Evelyn pursued her goal to achieve recognition for her dead brother.

Evelyn works in an office in Perry, and it was she who took on the job more or less of 'Master of Ceremonies' at the meeting. For somebody who had never done it before she was totally faultless. She had to cope with the whole event: the organising of it beforehand, setting out the hall, and making arrangements for the speakers. The Press was there too – there were three or four TV companies and the local newspapers.

Evelyn is a very good cook, but she is also something of a practical joker. She told me that she played a trick on some friends of hers and fed them wild raccoon for a meal. From then on I became extremely wary of everything I ate and it became quite a joke amongst us. I never did get raccoon, but every time I sat down I was convinced I was about to.

Another friend who had communicated with me in a similar way to Evelyn was Audrey Bigelow. Up until I had made contact with both of them I did not realise that they were very close. Audrey lost her brother in the Exercise too. When I was at her home, I looked out over the rear of her house and I heard something which annoyed them but which sounded fantastic to me. Every half hour you heard the hoot of the Union Pacific Railway thundering past and it was like music to my ears. This really was the heartland of the United States. And such hospitality! Each night they took me for dinner to a different member of the family. They paraded me literally all around their local town and everybody but everybody who came into contact with me seemed to introduce me to someone else. Even the local sheriff wanted his photograph taken standing next to me.

Before I went to Kansas, I had never met Audrey. When we arrived at the hall on the day of the meeting, there was this very tall and – I don't think she would mind me saying – very well-built lady standing in the entrance amongst a lot of other people. I just walked straight past her but she came up and said 'I'm Audrey'. She threw her arms around me and said she felt she had known me all of her life. She cried her eyes out. Then she gave me a plaque to thank me for what I had done for her brother.

For the meeting all the local people had banded together to make cakes, cookies and all the other things that they make in America. They had laid out on a table all sorts of photographs and newspaper clippings of the Exercise for people to look at. Among the relatives of the survivors and the friends, all intermingling there was this one Englishman. I was almost literally passed round from one to another and I became every bit as emotionally involved as they were. It was impossible not to be just as affected by the occasion. And when you get two or three very elderly people who lost men in that Exercise throwing their arms around you and weeping, it is too much for even the hardest of hearts. And I am certainly not a hard-hearted person.

When the meeting was called to order and everybody sat down, Evelyn introduced me and asked me to speak. My heart was in my mouth. I decided not to make a prepared speech. I just stood up on the stage for four or five minutes and spoke off the cuff. I must confess that I had to keep on swallowing because I felt the tears welling up. I remember I started the speech by saying that I left behind at Slapton Sands a beach full of yellow poppies. It was the first time the poppies had come out like that along the sands and I had been walking among them just before I left for the airport. It seemed fitting somehow.

I went on to talk for some 40 minutes about my own personal experiences, my beliefs about the Exercise and the men who died. At the end of it, the whole hall stood up and clapped and cheered. There were seven speeches altogether. Apart from me, there was Evelyn, there was a doctor and five survivors and before that a prayer was said by the local priest for everybody. After the meeting we met the TV and radio people and the journalists. One particular journalist picked up a comment I had made as a joke about being worried in case I found myself eating raccoon. He wrote a piece about it for his paper. Evelyn bought a copy of the newspaper and she laughed out loud when she found it mentioned raccoon. But she was really laughing because the joke was on me. I did not realise what she meant until I read the article in bed that night. In the paper, they described me as 'a podgy English gentleman with untidy grey hair and a classic English accent.' The photograph on the front page was a very big close-up of one side of my face, with me smoking a cigarette and looking decidedly unkempt. That was what Evelyn had been laughing at.

After the meeting a lot of the survivors and myself went back to Evelyn's home for a barbecue meal in the evening. That was a truly wonderful experience. We had the barbecue in the back yard. That area of Kansas is noted for its corn and soyabeans and it is also noted for hunting, tracking, shooting and fishing. Everywhere I looked the landscape seemed to go on and on for ever. It's no wonder they call it the Big Country. The whole family were there, children and grandchildren, brothers and sisters, and as I said the survivors. It was a huge get-together in Evelyn's back garden, with hundreds of photographs being taken.

Two of the survivors come to mind in particular. One is Dr Eugene Eckstam, who has made a considerable study of Exercise Tiger. He was a survivor and a doctor during the war. He made quite a long speech after I had sat down. But I have to say I think he spoke a lot about what people really did not want to hear. He was speaking from a doctor's point of view and told the audience that in his opinion as a doctor there was no way men could have stayed alive in that water for longer than 15 minutes. He added that they should not have removed their clothing or their boots when they were thrown into the sea. Apparently, that is something which men instantly think of doing. But the best medical advice is that the most important thing is to keep warm. He spoke about this at some length, and I must say he made me feel a bit uncomfortable. I realise he is a doctor and would know these things, but we were not talking about the Exercise from a clinical point of view. We were talking about young men between 17 and 21, whose ships had been torpedoed and who just wanted to get out to safety. And the first thing they thought of was to remove their boots – anything that might weigh them down in the sea – and jump for their lives.

During Exercise Tiger, Eugene Eckstam did everything right, as a doctor should do, and he survived. But still he was fortunate where other men were not.

But even if I did feel rather ill at ease with this very unemotional analysis of what they had done wrong, it should not detract from the fact that Eugene Eckstam himself is a fine man. He has drawn up a comprehensive list of survivors, and inspired by his work I made the suggestion at the meeting that during 1989 there should be one big meeting of all the men involved in Tiger: Navy, Army, relatives, brothers, sisters, mothers, fathers, friends. I suppose I thought it might be called 'A Farewell to Tiger', because a lot of these people are getting on in years now. Eugene supported the idea strongly and organising the event has now become a great challenge. Audrey and Evelyn suggested that an appropriate place would be Kansas or Missouri, in the very heart of America.

Evelyn Brannock's brother in one of the Quartermaster Divisions on the Exercise was on board one of the LSTs that was torpedoed and sunk. There were a number of other people there whose relatives were on the same vessel, and one Kansas lady told a story that was disturbing for Evelyn. Like her, she had lost her brother in the Exercise but had actually received his body back for burial in the States.

Evelyn having discovered he was in the same Quartermaster Division as her brother and Audrey Bigelow's brother and on the same vessel, naturally wanted to know why his body was returned and their brothers' were not. There could be a lot of reasons, the most obvious being where they all were on the ship at the time.

But another disturbing suggestion which I have not been able to confirm or rebut was made by one of the survivors of LST 517 – that the boat sank but was later recovered. It was apparently seen by this man in Southampton dockyard being repaired. This was the first time I had heard this theory and I don't really think anybody believed it as it was known that the bow of the ship was exposed above the surface for some time. I cannot believe that a few weeks before D-day they went to the trouble of salvaging an LST or taking it back to Southampton. Even though they were short of landing craft at the time, they surely could not have spared all the equipment needed for such an operation, let alone restored the vessel to a seaworthy state in the time available. But the man categorically stated he saw this vessel being repaired in Southampton dockyard.

It does not really make sense. After all, numbers are very easily confused. He probably did see an LST in Southampton, but 517, 527, 507, 572, all these numbers could become confused over the years. But Evelyn and the other relatives will naturally cling onto the faintest hope that their loved ones were found and were buried properly. My honest belief as far as that particular ship is concerned is that the men were all below deck at the time of the attack. The E-boat assault only lasted seven minutes and the ship went down in a very short space of time. I believe the men did not know a thing about it.

Evelyn is naturally concerned that her brother should have had a peaceful death. She did not like to think, nor did Audrey, that they had to suffer. That is a question we will never be able to answer. I hope for Evelyn's sake and for Audrey's sake and all the many hundreds of others that their loved ones did not suffer.

Since the war, Evelyn and Audrey have both tried to find out what had happened to their loved ones and all they met with was red tape, brick walls and negative answers. I suppose their appreciation for what I had done was tied up in the fact that all those years they had lived with the trauma of not knowing what had happened to their loved ones and I – as just an ordinary Englishman adopting that cause 18 years ago – had taken the whole story from A to Z and given them what they now know.

Audrey Bigelow's story was similar to that of Evelyn: she tried contacting all the official sources, but never got anywhere. This went on for many years and then when she picked up the newspaper article containing all the facts about what I had done she said it was like a message from God to her and she made immediate contact with me. It is the same for Audrey as it is for Evelyn. They did not get anywhere as far as American sources were concerned and I honestly believe that had I not done what I did they would still have been in the dark to this day.

They say so much in the letters and tapes they send me. They have peace of mind at last. They now know these men are listed on the Wall of the Missing at the Madingley Hill Cemetery in Cambridge – one of the most beautiful cemeteries on earth. I have given that to so many of them and I do not think I can give more

They are real characters, the people who live in Kansas. Apart from the business with the raccoon meat, they started telling me about doodle bugs. The only doodle bug I knew was the doodle bug that used to fly over the city I lived in during the war with the German V-rockets. but in Kansas they had doodle bugs that really were bugs – or beetles. They were nicknamed doodle bugs and they told me they lived under the ground and if I got a tin lid and tapped it and started calling 'Doodle bug, doodle bug' they would come up. I have to say that I was convinced that they were having me on and I was not going to accept this story at all.

Then Evelyn's elder brother Don came and said he had found some holes where doodle bugs were on his farm. It was evening time, so we all went out to see the bugs. I thought as I had not got much longer to stay here, I might as well see if it was true. In the dust in the barn, because it was so dry there, were these little tiny mounds, like miniature volcanic craters. They were not holes as such but they were that shape. I thought Don had perhaps been out with a stick and made a few of the holes. But then they all started getting down on their knees and calling, 'Doodle bug, doodle bug.' 'Silly buggers,' I thought. 'What are they doing?' But I thought I might as well join in. So I got a tin lid and I got down over three or four of these holes and started gently tapping the lid and calling, 'Doodle bug, doodle bug.' Then this thing which I could not see for soil and dust started moving upwards. You may have seen a worm moving just under the surface of the soil. The effect was much the same. It raises the soil up and you get a continuous mound as it moves forward, yet you cannot see it. I thought this could not be true, so I quickly scooped under it with my hand and up came a beetle-like bug. Within a few seconds, they were all coming out of their holes as we called them. I still cannot really believe it happened.

Don gave me a present which I treasured very much. It was from both him and his wife Nova. Nova has suffered a lot in her life. She has had cancer, and her left arm is totally useless. She and Don went down to the bottom of the garden and she dug up three roots of iris plants. She told me they were black irises, and she would like me to grow these and think of them always. They knew about my preference for black, and my habit of wearing black, and they thought this a fitting thing to do. I brought the irises home and planted them in my back garden. I have no doubt they will flourish.

Other fond memories are of meeting the different relatives of those who had been killed. Evelyn's son, Mark, who would have been Private Cottrell's nephew, was probably one of the cleverest hunters and trappers of the area and obviously a true Kansas lad. He took to me like a long lost friend – even the grandchildren came up to talk to me – everybody from little children to elderly adults.

When the visit was about to end, Evelyn and her husband Ron took me back out to Kansas City National Airport. We were waiting in the transit area in the departure lounge when who should turn up quite unexpectedly but Audrey Bigelow. Normally when I am in the departure lounge at an airport I am the first on the plane, but they just would not let me go. They literally clung onto me and I finally had to drag myself away, so emotional were the farewells. I was in no fit state to look out of the window of the plane but they were waving their wet handkerchiefs at me hoping I would see them as the plane took off. I left full of deep emotions and the hope that one day before too long I would return.

This was a trip I am very pleased to have made. On the way home I felt some sense of satisfaction at having given so many people something they wanted, I was just an ordinary Englishman, but they wanted my presence over there to thank me in person for what I had done.

The two plaques I have been given will always have a very special significance for me. Evelyn Brannock's shows a photograph of her brother and inscribed in the glass are his name and a picture of the tank and then in gold 'for grateful appreciation the family of Private James Oliver Cottrell wishes to acknowledge Ken Small for his unselfishness in giving his efforts in erecting a memorial commemorating the US soldiers during the pre-invasion off the shores of Slapton Sands on 28 April 1944. May God bless you. In loving memory of Private James Cottrell's parents Eleanor and Donovan Cottrell, Joe and Edith Newall and Junior and Codell Cottrell and Ron and Evelyn Brannock.'

Audrey Bigelow's says 'Mr Ken Small – in heartfelt appreciation for the giving of yourself in bringing all the due respect and honour to the men of Operation Tiger 1944 and peace of mind to their families. In memory of Private First Class Clarence Erwin Lasswell, by his loving family.'

I still hear regularly from the good friends I made in Perry, Kansas. Evelyn will send a tape, or Audrey will send a tape. They talk at length and ask me to look after myself; they feel as if they have known me all their lives. They know I started this thing through a nervous breakdown, and I think they have an inbuilt fear that I will overdo it and finish up with another one. So they have taken me unto themselves; they care what happens to me, and they cannot wait to hear from me. I know I have become very emotionally involved in this, but many other people, friends of mine, listen to these tapes and at the end there is no doubt everyone is tearful, such is the appreciation their messages show for what has been done for their lost loved ones. I find it difficult to play the tapes sometimes, because I know it is going to be such an emotional experience.

Evelyn started the ball rolling on this suggested meeting, because she had read an article in the newspaper about the Exercise and written in with details of her own experience. But the outcome has been much more than she expected. Her local newspaper took up the story and they published an article about Evelyn and about the loss of her brother and after that the correspondence and the telephone calls started to pour in from all over America – from survivors and from relatives. While I was at her home she pulled out a huge cardboard box and it was full of letters. She said they were all letters from people she had heard from since they read about her brother, from relatives, from survivors from friends and well-wishers. She has become an American focal point as I have become a focal point on the English side. She and I and people like Audrey are very closely linked now. We all find that the interest is enormous and wherever I go in America it is just the same. When I went before to Harrisburg, it was every bit the same. They are clamouring for information. They trust me, because I have done what I have done for no other motive than to respect and honour the loved ones that they lost during that Exercise.

Since the official memorial was put up in November 1987 I have had between 620 and 680 letters from America. In addition to that there are probably 50 or 60 from English people. They fill my study and overflow into the other rooms as well. They are split up into letters from relatives, from survivors and just well-wishers thanking me for what I have done. I have not yet counted those from survivors. I know there are a very substantial number and they have all been only too willing to let me have their own very graphic accounts. There have been one or two that have found great difficulty in putting it all down. Indeed, there is one that I have on tape who spoke to me through Audrey Bigelow about his experiences. He related to her what had happened and she put it all on tape and sent it to me. He was apologetic that there was no way that he could possibly have put it in writing.

It may seem strange but Exercise Tiger which happened so many years ago to them is as if it happened yesterday. I do not know whether English people feel the same way about it, but the Americans certainly do. Evelyn and Audrey were 10 or 12 year-old girls at the time their brothers were taken away. Those women, now in their fifties, are as moved now as on the day they saw their brothers leave never to come back.

I think they feel a mixture of emotions: sadness, grief, anger, frustration. I think also the fact that those men lost their lives on English territory, and they were the only Americans to do that, plays a great part in the emotional links many of the relatives and survivors still feel with Exercise Tiger.

I have no doubt that this emotional feeling of loss stems also from the fact that they never got the bodies back. They never knew what had happened to them. All they had received were telegrams saying that their men were killed in the European theatre of operations, no more than that. It is not like getting a telegram saying your brother was lost in action in Germany or wherever. It was not just anywhere, it was in England, during a practice exercise and because of the secrecy of it, they were just not told. People often class it as a cover-up, but my friend Manny Rubin and I put them right on that. It was never covered up; it was 'conveniently forgotten'.

One account I think puts it into a nutshell. It concerns a woman who lost her brother in the Exercise. On the night of 27 April 1944 this young man's mother woke up in the middle of the night screaming. She had had a nightmare in which her son appeared at the foot of the bed, dressed in a Roman Catholic priest's collar and said to her, 'I have to go, I have to go.' Her daughter quietened her down and told her nothing could happen to him, he was only in England. He died the very next day.

Another experience is only very recent. An American came to me and told me that he had lost his friend Billy in the Exercise. Ever since the war he had had this recurring dream which was haunting him: he was walking around a railway line and his friend Billy was coming towards him, but they never ever met. The American came over to England to try and find out what had happened to his friend and eventually arrived in Devon with me. I showed him that his friend had died during the Exercise and he cried and cried. Two weeks after his return to America I got a letter from him. Right across the page in capital letters was written, 'Ken Small you are the greatest man alive, the dream has now gone – at last Billy and I have met.'

12

THE MISSING GRAVES

'The bodies were beneath where we were standing.'

There is one particular aspect of Exercise Tiger which has aroused a great deal of comment and which I have kept separate from all the rest. My crusade has been to create a memorial for those who died that night. But in the course of my investigations it became clear that while they had certainly been forgotten by those in authority, some of them may also have been denied even a proper burial. All the survivors speak of seeing hundreds of corpses floating in the water the following morning. Some talk of the front ramp of a landing craft being used to scoop them up, although whether that could really be done without flooding the landing craft is another question. All the so-called bigoted officers were accounted for, so clearly there was a large-scale recovery operation for the bodies. But what happened to them after that? Eventually, many were interred at Madingley Hill near Cambridge. That much we know for certain.

Before that however, there are many stories of bodies being dumped in temporary graves in the immediate aftermath of the Exercise. It is a macabre thought, and not one I really like to talk about. But the question is whether any of the bodies were then just left in those temporary graves. For the relatives of those who died, the worst thought of all would be that their loved ones had not received a proper burial. There are strong suggestions that this may indeed be the case. But there has also been a lot of loose talk, which has only served to cloud the issue. The problem is sorting out possible fact from unconfirmed hearsay. I have spoken to or heard from only a few among the survivors from the American side who had anything to tell about the graves. One man was driving a bulldozer and was involved in actually digging the trenches in which the bodies were put temporarily. His letter made me shudder when I read it.

At the time the tank was recovered, a local lady, Dorothy Seekings of Stoke Fleming, revealed to the world's press that one day shortly after Exercise Tiger she was walking along a lane when an American lorry stopped and the man who was driving it gave her a lift. While driving he said he had to stop off at a field gate and unload something. When they stopped she stated she saw men digging and mounds of earth. She got out of the lorry and looking in the back she saw piles of bodies. During the period when Exercise Tiger had been taking place her father had been a baker and as a teenager she said she had special dispensation to be in the area to deliver bread to the troops. I must say, I found it a little difficult to understand why a small local baker would have the contract to supply the many hundreds and thousands of troops in the area. But the key question was, what about the bodies?

I was asked by a number of American veterans to try and confirm whether her story was true. So I spent many hours with Mrs Seekings. She told me that it was all perfectly true and she also said there was another American Army tank sunk near our beach. I asked her where it had gone down, and she said that it was off Blackpool Sands Beach, which is the beach immediately adjacent to Slapton Sands. She said it was not one of the swimming tanks, it was coming down a ramp off a landing craft and fell over the side into the water. I asked her how she could confirm this information. It turned out that one of her guests had been roped in to help. She had a house which took in a small number of paying guests and one particular guest was a fire-eater by profession and a subaqua club diver in his spare time. One day she had asked him to go out and find the tank. She told me that he did indeed find it, and what was more, while swimming among the weeds and the rocks, he found two complete human skeletons with dog tags around their necks and wrists.

This I found not merely difficult, but impossible to believe, on a storm-racked beach after 40 odd years. Also if the man's hobby was subaqua diving, and he had found either the tank or the skeletons, would he not have been experienced enough to have taken careful note of landmarks to rediscover the tank and the bodies? I asked Mrs Seekings what happened to the bodies. She replied that the coastguard came and took them away, and the fire-eating diver was sworn to secrecy. I later checked with the police and I checked with the coastguard and they totally denied it. I am quite prepared to believe the police in this case. At the end of the interview, I said to her, looking from her rear garden towards the sea, would she tell me approximately how far out to sea this tank was when it sank. She pointed to some trees which were about 200 yards away. Then obviously realising her mistake, said come to think of it, it must have been one of the swimming tanks, because you do not get a 200-yard long ramp coming off a landing craft. I have to admit that after that I have no great belief in that part of her story.

Mrs Seekings further stated that a friend of hers in Chillington, one of the villages that was evacuated, had a detached bungalow built after the war, and that while the foundations were being laid, the builders found a lot of human remains. The woman did not want any publicity, so she told the builders to carry on building the bungalow anyway. I asked Mrs Seekings how I could meet this woman. She replied that the woman used to go for her groceries each week to the cash and carry where Mrs Seekings' daughter worked in Kingsbridge. I suggested I could meet her there, and Mrs Seekings answered that she saw no reason why not. However, she again emphasised that the woman did not want publicity. I said I would respect her confidentiality but she said it might be better if she went along with me. I asked Mrs Seekings on numerous occasions for this interview, but nothing came of it. So in the end I thought I would ring up her daughter and ask her about the mystery woman.

I had in the meantime investigated the bungalow that had supposedly been built in Chillington but none of that type had been built. Then I spoke with Mrs Seekings' daughter, and asked if she would mind telling me about the lady who had found the human remains when having her bungalow built, and who came into her cash and carry every week. Her answer was very sharp and pert: the woman had not been in for three weeks; and she put the phone down. A week later Mrs Seekings telephoned me to say that she had got something for me. I went to her house, and on her dining room table there was an old polythene cooking salt jar with a red lid. I opened it, and the first thing I took out of it was a hand-written note in block capitals and unsigned which read, 'red soil from the Devon field where we all now rest in peace'. This I think was something made up to fob me off because I had been so insistent. It was difficult to believe it was anything other than a rather poor hoax.

Something else that was developing at this time was my relationship with the press – suddenly finding that more and more reporters were wanting to hear the story of the tank. The initial interest was limited, primarily because of all the publicity at the same time surrounding the visit of the queen and President Reagan to Normandy for the 40th anniversary of D-day, although the tank did get a lot of local TV and local press coverage. But once I started going to America and campaigning for the memorial service, the publicity increased. There were reporters from countries throughout the world and from all the main TV channels. The story of my campaign went right across America, Australia, Canada, New Zealand, Thailand, South Africa, Hong Kong, China, Israel, Sweden, Belgium, Denmark and Germany. Not only that, but there was coverage in the world's leading magazines like *Time*, *People Weekly* in America, *Der Spiegel* in Germany, and *Le Figaro* in France. For many weeks I was totally overwhelmed by the media; and in addition to that I had the guesthouse to run and guests to cook for. All the guests saw when they arrived was a temporary TV studio, day after day. As well as the foreign journals, all the British TV channels covered the story, and all the main daily newspapers. I had to appear on programmes like *TV-am*, programmes on Central Television in Birmingham, and broadcast on BBC World Service radio programmes all over the world.

One particular incident I remember is a visit by a Japanese reporter, who came to our house on a Sunday afternoon. He wanted to see me but insisted he would not disturb me on a

Sunday. So he came the following Wednesday, and spent two or three hours with me. His words at the end of the interview were, 'Mr Small, if you were in Japan you would be a very honoured gentleman.' And he left me £50 towards the cause. The German magazine *Der Spiegel* left £200. It is ironic that the only people to contribute were the Germans and the Japanese; all the rest were done for free.

I firmly believe that somehow or other, Dorothy Seekings got caught up in all the publicity surrounding the tank, and then found she could not back down. When she made the declarations in the first place, the field in which she stated the bodies were buried became the subject of worldwide attention. The farmer whose field it was threatened to use a shotgun on all the people who were invading it virtually every day. When I first met Mrs Seekings, her first words to me were that I must be making a lot of money out of that tank. I said I could assure her that not one single penny had come my way. But it was only a few weeks later that I spoke to two journalists who said Mrs Seekings had been demanding and getting £50.00 an interview for her information.

Perhaps the most difficult time for the two of us was when the TV people were trying to do a story about the tank and the bodies. I want to include just an extract from my diary at that time to show how the whole thing was starting to get out of proportion. The diary was written up by Sally Lucas one of the girls who was working at the guesthouse.

Tuesday, 13 October 1987
NBC left today. They are going to interview Seekings and Manny Rubin and the driver will pick up their gear later. Debbie Davies from Central came to say she will be filming at 3.00 pm Wednesday. She thoroughly believes Seekings and said everything Ken said about her was wrong.

Ken phoned Doug Mathias, Beverly Byron's aide. He said Central TV had been accusing Beverly of taking her father's side and covering up the fact that bodies were buried in tombs in Devon and are still there. Doug told Ken that Beverly would be the official government representative. Beverly and her party will also be staying here for the ceremony and the rest of her stay. Attlee [Wampler, commander of the tank] and Janet will also be staying here and they are bringing a sole survivor from a ship in Exercise Tiger with them. Attlee is still waiting for an official invitation from the council for the dinner at the Naval College.

Ken said he doesn't want to do the interview with Central if they upset Beverly and are taking Seekings' side in the matter. He told Manny about it and asked him not to do his interview either, but Manny has given his word. Manny said he would start the interview with 'Thank God for people like Beverly Byron.' Ken said they can just edit that out.

Wednesday, 14 October 1987

Ken phoned the boss of Central TV to complain about the way Beverly Byron was treated and Debbie Davies being so one-sided about Seekings' story. Kevin (her boss) said he thought Debbie was being a devil's advocate and playing one off against the other.

Ken was also put through to the researcher who spoke to Beverly Byron's representative. He told Ken he had sent Beverly some newspaper clippings about the Exercise and the fact that people still believe the men are still buried in concrete tombs around the area. The researcher apologised for upsetting Beverly. Kevin said they would phone Beverly's office and apologise to her for upsetting her. He also said he thought the whole story should be more to do with the Exercise blunder than with Seekings and the story about the bodies.

Kevin said the programme would be nothing without Ken's story and sixteen-year battle and could he come up to Birmingham on Friday, 23rd to be in the programme and answer questions.

4.15 pm Seekings phoned to ask if Central TV had been, Ken said no, why? She said she wasn't allowed to say until they had been, she had promised.

Half an hour later Ken phoned back to say they had been (they hadn't). Seekings said they told her Ken had said

> horrible things about her, she was a lying, awful woman, after the money etc., she asked Ken if they were still friends. Ken said yes.
>
> Ken phoned Central TV's boss, Kevin, to tell him what Debbie was up to. He said that he didn't know what she was playing at, unless she was playing one off against the other and it was up to Ken's discretion as to whether he does the interview or not. Ken asked if they had apologised to Beverly Byron yet. They said they could not get through to her office and could they have Doug Mathias' number instead.
>
> Debbie Davies and the camera crew came. Ken talked to her and Keith Hailey up in the office. Debbie said she was trying one up against the other, and she was sorry to have upset Ken. They had interviewed the farmer in whose field Seekings said the bodies were buried, and he had shot down Seekings' story. So had Ken. They just wanted to get the truth. Seekings was selling up and moving out of the area, would Ken still the do the story. Ken did it.'

I really think that Dorothy Seekings just found herself getting deeper and deeper into things and did not know what to do next. The TV people can be very insistent, and ordinary people, who are not used to that sort of pressure, just do not know what to do for the best. Mrs Seekings also told me another story about when she was driving her van around Slapton Ley at the time of Exercise Tiger and there was a big fire in the middle of the road made up of burning tyres. She stopped because she could not get through it, and several Americans approached her at pistol point. She was so frightened that she drove straight through this ball of fire and back home, regardless of being stopped. She had many many other similar stories, and really was extremely good at telling them. But in my opinion she was making many of them up.

I remember putting it into her head that if bodies had been recovered from the sea, they would have had dark green uniforms. Obviously if they were wet they would not be khaki, it would be more a dark green. Now, this was something she did not say initially. She did not talk about the bodies she saw having dark green uniforms. But after I mentioned it she always said that they did have dark green rather than khaki clothing. She stuck to that line at subsequent interviews, even though it was I who had said it, and not something she had originally recalled at all.

All the same, I should say that Dorothy Seekings is a nice woman and I liked her. She is quite stoutly built with slightly grey hair and very much Devonian in her character. I liked her but I was often upset by the macabre things she did. Once she took a relative of one of the dead Americans, a woman called Stella Rougley, to the field and said to her, 'Look, that is where your lost one is buried.' I thought that was too much, not least because I got the backlash of it. I had Stella Rougley and her family, including a present serving officer in the American Army, round at the guesthouse in a very distressed state, and it took me a lot of talking and a lot of convincing to make them believe that Mrs Seekings' story had a lot of holes in it and was probably not the truth. The farmer whose field it was had categorically stated that he was there before, during and after the Exercise, because the field was not within the actual boundaries of the Exercise. He swore that not one single blade of grass was ever disturbed in that field by the military.

However, that is far from the end of the matter of the bodies. It is a fact that bodies were buried locally. The holes in Dorothy Seekings' story appeared at a subsequent interview I had with an elderly man, who called me to his house. He is a retired farmer and he seemed to have no axe to grind. He had not spoken to the press, he did not ask for any money. What he did do was ask if he could get into my car, in order to show me something. With my help he got into the passenger seat. He was very discreet about it and would not even show his head above the level of the fascia. He gave me certain directions to follow. I followed them and when we got to a certain point he said ahead of us I would see a row of houses. I said I could see them. Ahead of the row of houses I would see a row of trees, of a type I will not mention here. I said I could see the trees as well. He then told me that was the field where the bodies were buried.

Dorothy Seekings was right, but she got the field wrong.

He also stated that he knew of a brick and concrete tomb holding bodies within about half a mile of where he and I were standing. Naturally, I asked him where it was. But he would not tell me. He said he had not even told his own sons. He said he could assure me that what he said was true, he even named the place where the bricks were made, at a point near Plymouth. I was not going to question him any further at that time, because it was clear he was not going to give me any more information.

Then about three weeks before June 1987, just before I was due to go to America he called me to his house again. He said he was getting very old and probably had not long to live, so he would show me where he firmly believed a lot of bodies were buried. Again he got into my car and we finished up in a field. We went into the field and walked some 60 to 80 yards. Then he said beneath where we were standing there were two brick and concrete air raid shelters with steps leading down to them. The bodies were in those shelters and the steps had been blown up to seal them off.

It was a strange feeling. Around the area where we stood were all sorts of patches of concrete. One does not expect to find concrete in the middle of a field. There were concrete slabs, bricks, concrete blocks, but all in different patches. Some of the concrete was covered with grass and I suppose if you had taken off a layer of grass, you would have seen a lot more concrete. It was an eerie sensation.

How did he come to know the bodies were there? The answer is that he was a farmer in that area during the war, and was evacuated. He returned to the district very quickly after the whole thing had happened. I would not categorically state that I believe him. Nor would I categorically state that I disbelieve him. All I know is that when I stood on that spot, I got a very strange feeling. Men were buried locally and it has been stated by American historians that there is a possibility that men may still be buried in local fields.

When the men were killed in the area it was obvious that they should be buried. It was fast approaching D-day and expediency was essential. They had not the time, nor probably anything else, to make sure these men received their proper military burials. There was also the fact that the Exercise was extremely secret. So a lot of the men were buried within the confines of the Exercise area as a temporary measure. The American authorities have always stated ever since that these men were subsequently exhumed and buried in a local cemetery in Surrey and subsequently at Madingley Hill in Cambridge, or taken back to America. I know that a lot of bodies were taken back to America. I know that a lot of bodies were marked and buried in Madingley Hill Cemetery in Cambridge, the US cemetery. I know there are huge numbers on the Wall of the Missing. I know there were many many bodies buried initially at a cemetery in Surrey. But I still think that one has got to say it is highly likely that some – albeit a few – did get left behind in the fields of Devon.

The strange part about it is that I have been able to find literally hundreds of documents relating to the Exercise itself – it is chronicled almost minute by minute – but there are virtually no records of the disposal of the bodies. I think that silence speaks volumes; but what I have been able to find out is even more disturbing. I have two lists of names of men showing that they were buried at Brookwood Cemetery in Surrey and also in Cambridge. The point is that these men are first shown as being buried at Madingley Hill, Cambridge on 28 April. There are both Army and Navy personnel on the list, and they come from a number of different LSTs. In all there are about 100 names. But how could they have been buried in Cambridge only hours after being pulled from the sea in Devon? Then, on another official list, the same names appear as being buried in Brookwood Cemetery between 1 and 3 May. Why would they have been moved? I think it is impossible that those men were moved to Madingley so quickly, nor does it make any sense to disinter them and move them to Brookwood, when their names are still recorded at Madingley. I think the two lists prove that a number of bodies were moved around, and either deliberately or by accident officialdom lost track of them. I know of at least one case where a man listed as buried in Cambridge is also listed as lost in Normandy. Immediately after the Exercise, senior officers wanted those bodies buried and forgotten – that much is certain.

But I say now, as I said when I first went to the field where I believe some bodies still lie, that I will not disclose the whereabouts of this particular place. I cannot honestly see after all this time any useful purpose being served. If the men were buried there we know that they were buried temporarily. But if there are any bodies still in the area, there would almost certainly be no identification marks on them. It most certainly would not do the relatives any good. Devon is a very beautiful area, and if they are there now they should be left to rest in peace for ever more, in the safe knowledge that their sacrifice has been broadcast worldwide and they have proper and appropriate memorials to mark their deaths.

I would not want to be the prime mover in any campaign to try and trace them although the American Government's policy – as stated categorically to me – was that in the event of any further evidence of any of their men being buried in fields abroad being found, then they would have these men exhumed and they would receive proper burials. I believe them, but I do not think that is what should happen, after more than 40 years. I fought for 18 years to get these men recognised and a memorial raised to them, and I do not want to be involved in any macabre search for skeletons.

As for Mrs Seekings, she is now leaving the area. I know that some months ago her property was on the market. I just wish that she had not categorically stated to the relatives that their men were buried in those fields. Had it been true, there was the possibility of the Americans subsequently exhuming them and subsequently returning them. She said that to her knowledge they had never been exhumed. She knew this because, as she puts it in her own words, 'I often pass that field.' But how often is often, and how long does it take to exhume bodies? Could it be that Mrs Seekings had not gone back to that field for two or three or four days at a time or even a week? I must admit in view of the other stories she has told me I find this one very difficult to believe.

As for the motives of the retired farmer. There were no motives, that was the strange thing about this incident. He did not ask me for money, he was not interested in money. In the first instance he told me he had not even told his sons. At our second meeting he told me it was because he did not have long to live and there was no reward whatever in the revelation. I found him to be a kindly, sincere, infirm elderly man. I respected him and I cannot see any reason why he should tell me other than wanting me to know the truth. I stick to that to this day. There is no sure way of knowing, though, short of exhumation, which I do not want to happen.

13

THE NEXT CRUSADE

'If I had all the time over again, there is nothing I would do differently.'

When I started writing this book, I had intended it to end with my trip to the reunion in Perry, Kansas, and my thoughts on the whereabouts of the bodies. It brought my story almost up to date, apart from a few reflections on what I might do next. But as when I had my nervous breakdown, fate played a part in my life again. Partly because of the tank, things have changed in a way I could never have foreseen, and my story has not the tidy ending I had intended. Perhaps it was an omen, but when I arrived back at the airport from the meeting in Kansas, I had the first shock. I had just got on the coach when the woman sitting next to me collapsed and died. I felt a bit depressed anyway after having been through such an emotional experience in the United States, and the sudden death of that unknown woman affected me greatly. When I arrived home everything seemed fine at first. Then after a day or two, my whole personal life seemed to blow up.

Sally Lucas had helped me over five years with this story. Contrary to what some people believe we had a caring relationship and nothing more involved than that. While I was in Kansas she made regular phone calls to me to check that I was all right, which boosted my confidence a lot. But my wife started to show signs of extreme jealousy. Sally, who had helped me so much over the trauma of the tank, had opted to move away from the guesthouse and had acquired a bed sit. My wife wanted a divorce. Solicitors were involved and I was under pressure to admit that I had committed unreasonable behaviour in two respects: firstly, that Sally, albeit innocently, had worked closely with me for five years, which had caused extreme distress to my wife, and secondly in the divorce petition was cited my involvement with the memorial and with the tank as being time I had spent to the neglect of my wife.

This hurt me greatly. I had done all the things I did for the memory of the dead Americans and for no other reason. On the other hand I could not accept the idea that apart from the question of Sally, who had done for me nothing but good, and with whom my relationship was innocent, I was faced with a divorce petition citing a Sherman tank as co-respondent. However, the divorce is going through. For several weeks I suffered severe trauma. I could not understand why it was all happening now. It seemed that I had spent all these years sorting out the tragedy of these young Americans only to finish up with an enormous tragedy in my own life.

When the tank was quoted in the divorce documents, it was extremely distressing. I admit I devoted 18 years to it but I do not regret what I did. I cannot regret what I did. I may have sacrificed my personal life but I would do it again.

It is true that the tank did become an obsession. But I do not think I went too far. Every American I have spoken to has left me in no doubt that it has all been more than worthwhile. It is a sacrifice I had to make. When Americans visit me in tears with a story of a lost relative I know I could not have changed the course of my life.

One such story concerned a young American sailor, who was 16 years old. He volunteered to join the American Navy, and he lied about his age. He was 16 and should have been 17. He came over to Slapton, changed his mind and asked for a discharge. His commanding officer told him that by the time his discharge papers came through he would be 17 anyway, so he might as well stay on. He died during Exercise Tiger. He was 17 on 27 April 1944 and he died on 28 April 1944. He had had just one legal day in the American Navy.

When I hear stories like that, I cannot regret anything I have done, no matter who I lose, no matter what sacrifice to my own personal life there may be. I sincerely regret the distress caused to my wife; I want to help her but I must be free to see this whole thing through right to the end, free to do as I see fit. It is fair to say that I ignored almost everything else in my life other than the tank. Obsession is the word I have used, but I also think it was a crusade. The early stages and the events that led up to it indicate to me that I was chosen to do it. It had to be. I have suffered substantial financial losses because of all this. I have had no desire for financial gain. I have been impelled only by the thought of so many forgotten men, and of their relatives in America who could not forget them and had failed to find out more of their death.

Recently I heard from two US Army colonels, who became colonels in the 1960s. Both these men told me they survived the Exercise. But when they reached the rank of colonel and started to try and find out why it had gone wrong, they were both officially told to shut up.

Coach loads of American tourists frequently come to the tank and often I am asked to talk to them. It is becoming ever more difficult to start talking about it, because it brings a huge lump to my throat, knowing the tragedy that I have uncovered and also the tragedy it has created in my own life. But I feel I must talk to them and to the thousands of English people who are also extremely interested. On a recent occasion I had just finished talking to an American coach load of veterans and tourists when, on my way out of the car park, I was stopped by three coach drivers of English visitors from Yorkshire. I had to go from coach to coach and talk to them as well and they were just as fascinated as the Americans had been. In only a few days time I have to go down there again. A coach load of American veterans is arriving, bringing with them a preacher to hold a service at the tank. I am to be with them during this service.

When survivors see the tank for the first time a frequent reaction is tears. Flowers and wreaths are then placed on the tank and afterwards they individually take bunches of flowers to the beach to scatter on the sea. It means so much to these people. How on earth could I let them down? I have become the centre of something I never even dreamed about in those early days when I started.

They ask me questions about bodies or what happened to them. Though many of their questions cannot be answered with certainty, they show sheer heartfelt appreciation for my giving peace of mind to them at long last. So many have accepted what has happened to their loved ones because of what I have done. All these years they have not been able to do that and their appreciation has no bounds. Looking back, if I had the time all over again there is nothing I would do differently.

The main lesson I learnt over the 20 years was that there is a lot of very deep human feeling for people that are lost in World War II and that still goes on. The lesson I have learnt in my own private life is that there has been a sacrifice to pay and I have had to pay it. But when I look at my private life and I think of what I have given to those countless Americans there is no comparison. If someone had told me that in 20 years time I would do what I set out to do but my private life would be ruined, I would do it again without hesitation.

But whatever my personal problems, the questions that still remain are the questions concerning the attitudes of the officials I encountered along the way. Until I actually recovered the tank, there was a lot of opposition from all sources in America to my buying it and I pulled through all that. In the period from recovering the tank to fighting for the official memorial, it is fair to say that every department in the Pentagon was helpful; the secretary of defence, secretary for the Navy, secretary for the Army, Congress all answered my requests. I never got a no, not even to the request for a letter from the president.

That was the ultimate thank you letter – the one from Ronald Reagan. I thought that I had reached the top when I got a bill through Congress, or rather when Beverly Byron got it through for me. But in the course of my campaign I had telephoned the White House dozens of times, and even written – which is not something I usually did – and one day a letter arrived in a huge envelope, made of parchment not paper. It is simply headed: The White House, Washington DC 12 April 1988.

> On behalf of all Americans, thank you for your kind and generous efforts in helping to establish a memorial at Torcross England, honoring the great American soldiers and service men who died in 1944, during a rehearsal for the D-

> day landings of World War II. Your concern for our servicemen who made the surpreme sacrifice exemplifies the strong bonds of friendship and admiration which unite the people of our countries. This memorial has strengthened those bonds by reminding us of the untold sacrifice in contributions of citizens such as yourself who endure countless hardships for a common cause. The tragic loss of lives in April 1944 bitterly reminds us that freedom is not free, but requires the steadfast courage and dedication of many who are willing to fight to safeguard that freedom, solely for the men to arise today like those in 1944, and stand ready to defend freedom. Your compassion serves as an inspiration not only to them but to all those who cherish freedom throughout the world. God bless you.

It is signed by the President of the United States.

But if the American attitude changed, the British did not. There has always been a lack of interest from the British side. I knew well that 32 British Navy vessels had been involved in this Exercise, and it was the district council's wish and my own that the representation of the English side at the memorial ceremony, and at the dinner at the Britannia Royal Naval College to welcome the American delegation, should be significant. It was a great disappointment to both the district council and myself that the secretary of defence, our MP, the Lord Lieutenant of Devon, the flag officer, Plymouth were unable to accept our invitations.

The official disinterest extended to supplying written details as well. In my investigations there is a wealth of documentary evidence that has come from the States, and virtually nothing from the British side. I researched the English naval side of this Exercise and found the names of the ships that were involved in the Exercise. Most of them have now been scrapped and some were sold to India and Pakistan and other countries. Nearly all the logbooks were gone. The only one which appeared was by coincidence. I had a letter from a man called Mr Hiscock, who ever since the war had been telling people that he was on board a heavy cruiser shelling England with live ammunition.

He said in his letter that people had virtually dubbed him a crank. How could an English cruiser be shelling England? He expressed the hope that perhaps people might believe him now. In my researches I had uncovered the one and only logbook available – which was for his ship HMS *Hawkins*. It describes how HMS *Hawkins* left Plymouth and spent 45 minutes shelling Slapton before the Exercise. As Mr Hiscock said, 'We created hell on shore.'

On board the *Hawkins* were English Marines watching the shore as the young Americans were landing. On the beaches they had a white tape line beyond which the Americans should not cross until the live firing had finished. But the Marines said they were going straight through the white tape line and getting blown up. So Hiscock's story turned out to be true, and it was proved by the only log I ever uncovered.

Nor was the Army much more helpful than the Navy. I have related how the Army at first promised help, and then pulled out at the last moment in a way which might have stopped all chance of bringing the tank ashore. But that was not the only example of military disinterest. I had a visit from a regimental sergeant major, who in the 1960s was an instructor at Sandhurst. He categorically stated to me that Exercise Tiger was used at Sandhurst as an example of how not to carry out an exercise. But when a friend of mine in the Army approached Sandhurst to find out more, they denied all knowledge of it. I believe the regimental sergeant major; he had no reason not to tell the truth. At least the appreciation for the memorial from ordinary English people has been every bit as great as from the American people. There have been as many tears shed by English people over those lost young men as there were by the Americans.

Sometimes I go down to the tank and try to be incognito. I pull up my car near the tank and I wind the window down. There is always someone there, sometimes you can hardly see the tank for people and it has been like that for the past four years and more. I listen to ordinary English people talking about it and saying 'Good gracious me all these young men were killed' and 'What a shame'. It moves everybody, young and old. I do not know whether they should feel angry, I think it is a bit too late for anger. But I like to think that they feel some compassion for those young men who came over here to help us in a very very difficult situation in those years of World War II.

An elderly lady came only a week ago from Torquay with her husband, and she said, 'Ken Small you are a lovely fella,' and she put her arms round me and gave me a kiss. She said that she had had a mandolin since the war with a very special significance. On it were inscribed the names of the men of the crew of the LCT 639 who landed on Omaha Beach in Normandy on 6 June 1944. Many of those men were billeted with her in Torquay. She told me that all these years since, she had been looking for a home for this little mandolin and now that she had met me, this was the home it should have. It was a real piece of history, and a treasure to this elderly English woman, who quite willingly parted with it to me and was prepared to say that this was the home it had been looking for all these years.

One day obviously some of the memories will fade a little. But they will fade in the safe knowledge that those young men who died were not forgotten. They have their memorial. They have also received worldwide publicity, which was long overdue. Now I would like to see the survivors and relatives of the Exercise who are alive today receive a special medal. To quote but one example, there is Colonel Stanley Stout, the man who had the courage and thought to shoot through the cable that was jamming the lifeboat and saved 25 young American lives. People like that deserve some tangible recognition from the American Government. I think the least they could now do is to create a specially struck medal to give to the survivors and to the relatives of all those men who died. They were forgotten, they are now not forgotten, and it would be fine if they could receive such a reminder officially. That is the next Ken Small crusade to campaign that each of those people should receive a specially struck medal.

World War II will never disappear completely from people's

memory. The tank is one reminder. I think it will survive me, it is a very solid object. I would like to be remembered as somebody who cared for so many young men who gave their lives so that we might live today in freedom and that they would never be forgotten. Many men lost their lives in World War II but these men lost their lives off the coast of England before the invasion of Europe had even started. I care about them now and I will go on caring about them in the future.

I will never understand why the Americans erected in 1954 an obelisk on Slapton Sands to thank the local people of five villages for vacating their homes but made no mention on it of the loss of so many lives. Obviously at the time it was necessary for the affair to be kept secret. It had to be so. But as the years wore on, it became more and more unnecessary. The man in charge of all operations at that time was General Eisenhower and Exercise Tiger does not appear in his memoirs. I often wonder why, because it was a major event. However, General Eisenhower subsequently became president of the United States. So does that raise any questions? It was certainly very conveniently forgotten.

There can be no better dedication for a book that has involved me in so much time, so many heartaches and so many tears than to list the names of the men killed and to show the relatives that each individual one is mentioned. Many of the names are at the Madingley Hill Cemetery in the Wall of the Missing. But I feel it is right to list the names of each one here. I know from my own personal experiences that each person who sees the name of a loved one, on what is really a roll of honour at the back of the book, will feel proud that after all these years they have made history. I know one woman who lost her brother when he was only 18. She said he would never have dreamed that he would be mentioned in such a book and he would have been very proud. It has taken many many years, but his name will now be remembered with the rest of them.

AFTERWORD

The crews were bone-weary after months of practice landings. Exercise Tiger seemed to be another step in the preparation for the assault on Europe.

The attack was sudden and unexpected. The E-boats' torpedoes struck viciously again and again. Their deck firing was devastating and cruelly beautiful, sending up arching incendiary colours. We could *feel* the screams of our comrades in the burning waters astern. We shook with fear and anger. Why were we so helpless and unprotected? Why were we dying so horribly, in these lonely, cold faraway waters?

Over 40 years later, those memories were buried in deep recesses of our minds. The survivors were scattered across the vastness of America, submerged in their day-to-day existence. But lurking in the background, were so many unanswered questions. Unknown to all of us, the veil of secrecy was being lifted.

Against all odds, battering against military and bureaucratic closed doors, an Englishman, Ken Small, devoted his energies, time and financial resources to getting the answers. Most important of all, he exacted the tribute and acknowledgements of the sacrifices of those wonderful men who took part in Exercise Tiger.

Manny Rubin
Ex-signalman LST496

ROLL OF HONOUR

This list gives the names of those I have been able to discover who were killed or missing in action during Exercise Tiger. The list is as comprehensive as my researches have permitted:

ARMY CASUALTIES

Ovid C. Adcock	Pvt	3206th QM Sv Co
Alvin E. Aid	Pfc	3206th QM Sv Co
Marvin R. Alexander	Pfc	607th QM GR Co
Walter M. Alexander	Pvt	557th QM RH Co
John J. Allen	T/5	478th Amph Trk Co
Delmar R. Allen	Cpl	3206th QM Sv Co
Albert F. Alsip	T/5	462d Amph Trk Co
Sam S. Arcuri	T/5	478th Amph Trk Co
Joe M. Arismendiz	Pfc	3206th QM Sv Co
Marion J. Asberry	Pvt	3206th QM Sv Co
Raymond (NMI) Baldwin	Pvt	3206th QM Sv Co
Calvin C. Banister	Sgt	3206th QM Sv Co
Ralph E. Barber	Pvt	3206th QM Sv Co
Chester (NMI) Barrett	S/Sgt	557th QM RH Co
Edwin A. Basgall	Pfc	3206th QM Sv Co
William R. Battle	Pvt	557th QM RH Co
James R. Baugus	Pvt	3206th QM Sv Co
Carl M. Bean	Pfc	625th Ord (Am) Co
Walter B. Bergfeld	Pvt	3206th QM Sv Co
John (NMI) Bernardo	Pvt	33d Chem Decon Co
Nilo V. Bertini	Pfc	33d Chem Decon Co
Howard G. Bird	Pvt	3206th QM Sv Co
Louis L. Birkley Jr.	Pvt	3206th QM Sv Co
Martial J. Bisaillon	T/5	531st Engr Shore Regt
Floyd E. Blake	T/4	557th QM RH Co
Thomas J. Blethroad	Pfc	3206th QM Sv Co
Harley E. Blevins	Pfc	3206th QM Sv Co
Frederick W. Blind	Pvt	478th Amph Trk Co

William (NMI) Blond	Pvt	557th QM RH Co
Jacob A. Bohl	Pvt	557th QM RH Co
Louis A. Bolton	Sgt	607th QM GR Co
Bernard E. Bonderer	Cpl	3206th QM Sv Co
Harvey J. Borchers	Pfc	531st Engr Sh Regt
Winford G. Bost	Pvt	3206th QM Sv Co
Hoy F. Boyles	Pvt	3206th QM Sv Co
Portter J. Bratton	Pvt	3206th QM Sv Co
Calvin D. Brecheisen	T/5	3206th QM Sv Co
Wayne R. Brewer	Pfc	531st Engr Sh Regt
Edward L. Brown	Pvt	557th QM RH Co
George E. Brown	T/5	557th QM RH Co
Ivan J. Brown	Pvt	3206th QM Sv Co
John B. Brown	Pvt	478th Amph Trk Co
John W. Brumfield	Pvt	33d Chem Decon Co
Donald S. Bryant	Pfc	531st Engr Sh Regt
Ernest C. Bryson	Pvt	3206th QM Sv Co
George W. Buckner	Pfc	3206th QM Sv Co
Robert E. Burke	Pfc	3206th QM Sv Co
Floyd H. Burks	Pvt	3206th QM Sv Co
Harold W. Burns	Pvt	3206th QM Sv Co
Robert T. Burrell	Pfc	3206th QM Sv Co
Metro (NMI) Butry	Pvt	3206th QM Sv Co
Jay H. Cain	Cpl	3206th QM Sv Co
Paul J. Caldwell	Pvt	3206th QM Sv Co
John H. Callahan	Pfc	3206th QM Sv Co
Terrence V. Campbell	Pvt	557th QM RH Co
William M. Campbell	Pfc	557th QM RH Co
Dominick (NMI) Caracciolo	Pfc	697th QM GR Co
Ernest (NMI) Carey	Pvt	3206th QM Sv Co
Georgie P. Cates	Pvt	3206th QM Sv Co
Ulysses J. Catman	Pvt	478th Amph Trk Co
James P. Cavanaugh	Pvt	557th QM RH Co
Libro C. Cesaro	Pvt	3206th QM Sv Co
Richard L. Chamberlain	Pvt	3206th QM Sv Co
Robert G. Chambers	Pvt	3206th QM Sv Co
Donald H. Childs	S/Sgt	3206th QM Sv Co
Arthur F. Chudzinski	Pvt	3206th QM Sv Co
Joseph (NMI) Ciccio	Cpl	3206th QM Sv Co
Ott S. Circle	Pvt	3206th QM Sv Co
John J. Clardy	T/5	462d Amph Trk Co
Herman D. Clark	Pfc	3206th QM Sv Co
Kenneth (NMI) Clayton	Pvt	33d Chem Decon Co
Francis M. Coan	Pvt	3206th QM Sv Co
Guy (NMI) Coleman	Pfc	557th QM RH Co
Robert J. Conklin	T/5	462d Amph Trk Co

Willie J. Conner	Pvt	557th QM RH Co
Woodson D. Constant	Pvt	3206th QM Sv Co
Robert M. Cooke	Pvt	478th Amph Trk Co
Christopher T. Cope	Pfc	3206th QM Sv Co
James O. Cottrell	Pvt	3206th QM Sv Co
Arthur L. Craig	Pvt	557th QM RH Co
Harold E. Crandell	Pvt	3206th QM SV Co
Carrell S. Crane	Pvt	3206th QM Sv Co
Poindexter D. Crawford	Pfc	557th QM RH Co
Thomas C. Creed Jr	Cpl	3206th QM Sv Co
Ed W. Crocker	Pvt	3206th QM Sv Co
Allesantro (NMI) Cutrone	T/5	462d Amph Trk Co
Samuel J. Cut	T/5	478th Amph Trk Co
Stephen J. Czyzniak	T/5	462d Amph Trk Co
Nick G. Dakis	Pvt	607th QM GR Co
Homer L. Dame	Cpl	3206th QM Sv Co
Leroy (NMI) Daniels	Pvt	818th Port Bn
Fred S. Danner	Pfc	3206th QM Sv Co
Thomas (NMI) Daoukas	Pfc	3206th QM Sv Co
Bernard A. Davenport	Sgt	478th Amph Trk Co
Franklin W. Davis	Pfc	3206th QM Sv Co
Clarence O. Deakyne Jr	S/Sgt	33d Chem Decon Co
Morris J. Debaene	Cpl	3206th QM Sv Co
Paul R. DeHass Jr	Sgt	3206th QM Sv Co
Edward J. Delamater	Ist Lt	607th QM GR Co
Anastacio (NMI) DeLeon	Pfc	556th QM RH Co
John A. Delitko	Pfc	625th Ord (Am) Co
Michael J. DePasquale	2d Lt	557th QM RH Co
Joseph F. DeSalvo	T/5	3206th QM Sv Co
Paul J. Dindino	T/5	478th Amph Trk Co
Troy (NMI) Dobson	Pfc	557th QM RH Co
Alexander G. Donaldson	T/4	625th Ord (AM) Co
Garland W. Donaldson	Pvt	3206th QM Sv Co
Earl V. Douglas	Pvt	3206th QM Sv Co
John M. Douglas Jr	T/5	3206th QM Sv Co
Oscar L. Drawdy Jr	T/5	462d Amph Trk Co
Frank (NMI) Dubisz	Pfc	478th Amph Trk Co
Meredith J. Duckworth	Pfc	3206th QM Sv Co
Johnnie O. Duncan	Pvt	3206th QM Sv Co
William A. Duncan	Pvt	3206th QM Sv Co
Quong J. Dye	Pfc	557th QM RH Co
Ralph T. Earnest	Pvt	3206th QM Sv Co
Roy E. Eckhoff	Pfc	3206th QM Sv Co
Mathews J. Edelman	Pvt	3206th QM Sv Co
Bill E. Edwards	Pvt	3206th QM Sv Co
John J. Edwards	Pfc	531st Engr Sh Regt

Herman (NMI) Eintracht	Pvt	557th QM RH Co
Carl M. Elliott	Pvt	3206th QM Sv Co
William R. Elliott	Pfc	531st Engr Sh Regt
Nicholas J. Evangelist	S/Sgt	3206th QM Sv Co
Junior T. Farris	Pfc	3206th QM Sv Co
Darrell D. Ferguson	Pvt	3206th QM Sv Co
Edwin G. Fischer	Pvt	557th QM RH Co
David E. Fizer	Pvt	3206th QM Sv Co
Herman (NMI) Fleming	T/5	478th Amph Trk Co
Arthur A. Fletewall	Pfc	3206th QM Sv Co
Charles R. Floyd	Pvt	3206th QM Sv Co
Lawrence R. Flynt	T/5	462d Amph Trk Co
William J. Follmer	Pfc	557th QM RH Co
Russell (NMI) Fontana	Pvt	462d Amph Trk Co
Adrian L. Ford	Pvt	3206th QM Sv Co
Salvadore D. Ford	Pfc	462d Amph Trk Co
Harold G. Foster	Pfc	818th Port Bn
Joseph H. Frank Jr	Pvt	3206th QM Sv Co
Richard L. Franks	Pvt	625th Ord (AM) Co
Hershel G. Freed	Pvt	3206th QM Sv Co
Leslie W. Friend	Pfc	3206th QM Sv Co
Joseph A. Galuppi	Pvt	3206th QM Sv Co
Eugene (NMI) Gamer	Pfc	462d Amph Trk Co
Lester J. Gardner	Pvt	531st Engr Sh Regt
William A. Garrison	T/5	462d Amph Trk Co
Herbert S. Garvin	2d Lt	625th Ord (AM) Co
John J. Gasser	Pfc	3206th QM Sv Co
Walter F. Gearhart	Cpl	625th Ord (AM) Co
Donald E. Gephart	Pfc	3206th QM Sv Co
Hilmer L. Gieschen	Pfc	3206th QM Sv Co
Bill E. Gillespie	Pfc	3206th QM Sv Co
John P. Glass	T/5	557th QM RH Co
John W. Glasscock	Pvt	3206th QM Sv Co
Melvin R. Glaze	Pvt	3206th QM Sv Co
Shirley C. Godsey	T/5	557th QM RH Co
Louis J. Golfinopoulos	Pfc	3206th QM Sv Co
John J. Gonshirski	Pvt	557th QM RH Co
Dennie (NMI) Goss	Pvt	3206th QM Sv Co
James P. Gray	Pfc	3206th QM Sv Co
William H. Gray	Pvt	462d Amph Trk Co
John C. Grevon	S/Sgt	607th QM GR Co
Roy B. Grisby	Pvt	478th Amph Trk Co
Harold H. Grossman	T/5	478th Amph Trk Co
Marvin W. Groves	T/5	3206th QM Sv Co
Dale E. Guffin	Cpl	3206th QM Sv Co
Francis L. Haile	Pfc	3206th QM Sv Co

John P. Hanks	Pfc	557th QM RH Co
Ern F. Harrington	Pvt	3206th QM Sv Co
Frank G. Harrison Jr	T/4	625th Ord (AM) Co
Ernest P. Haynes	Pvt	557th QM RH Co
Peter J. Heffernan	Pvt	3206th QM Sv Co
Eugine A. Henley	Pfc	462d Amph Trk Co
Ravila (NMI) Herbert	Pvt	607th QM GR Co
Charles W. Hobbs	2d Lt	462d Amph Trk Co
Lester (NMI) Hobbs	Cpl	3206th QM Sv Co
Alvie M. Hogland	Pfc	557th QM RH Co
Otis L. Hollon	Pfc	3206th QM Sv Co
Robert E. Holmes	Sgt	607th QM GR Co
Stephen G. Holzberger Jr	Pfc	462d Amph Trk Co
George E. Hoops	Pvt	1605th Engr Map Depot
Robert L. Hopkins	T/5	3206th QM Sv Co
Albert H. Hovis	Pvt	3206th QM Sv Co
Francis L. C. Hudson	Pfc	3206th QM Sv Co
Anton W. Huelsmann	Pvt	607th QM GR Co
Merle B. Humble	T/5	478th Amph Trk Co
William L. Humphrey	Pfc	3206th QM Sv Co
Arnold (NMI) Hurt	Pvt	3206th QM Sv Co
Clifford E. Hutchison	Pfc	3206th QM Sv Co
Richard H. Jensen	T/5	462d Amph Trk Co
Horace (NMI) Johnson	Pvt	33d Chem Decon Co
James G. Johnson	Pvt	462d Amph Trk Co
John T. Johnson	Cpl	557th QM RH Co
Claude E. Johnston	Pfc	557th QM RH Co
Everett W. Jordan	Pvt	531st Engr Sh Regt
Raymond O. Joyal	T/5	478th Amph Trk Co
John A. Kapinos	Pvt	531st Engr Sh Regt
William M. Kay	Pfc	3206th QM Sv Co
Otto W. Keller	Pvt	3206th QM Sv Co
George A. Kielbasa	Pfc	3206th QM Sv Co
William E. King	Pfc	3206th QM Sv Co
Bertram (NMI) Kinkead	Pfc	3206th QM Sv Co
Johnny D. Kladus	Pvt	3206th QM Sv Co
John T. Klobe	Cpl	3206th QM Sv Co
Elmer L. Knight	Pfc	557th QM RH Co
William (NMI) Korodi	Pvt	3206th QM Sv Co
Ezra F. Kreiss	S/Sgt	3206th QM Sv Co
Salvatore (NMI) LaIacona	1st Lt	Hq, 1st Engr Sp Brigade
Douglas L. Lambert	Pfc	557th QM RH Co
Walter V. Larson	Pvt	3206th QM Sv Co
Clarence E. Lasswell	Pfc	3206th QM Sv Co
Harold E. Lee	T/4	478th Amph Trk Co
Robert B. Leishman	T/5	462d Amph Trk Co

John H. Levengood	Pvt	462d Amph Trk Co
Champ W. Libla	Pfc	3206th QM Sv Co
Rocco F. Lillo	Pvt	531st Engr Sh Regt
Evan W. Long	Pvt	3206th QM Sv Co
Joseph D. Long	Pvt	3206th QM Sv Co
Samuel S. Loper	T/5	462d Amph Trk Co
Joseph P. LoPresto	Pfc	557th QM RH Co
Blaine L. Louder	Pfc	3206th QM Sv Co
Theodore G. Lowell	T/5	531st Engr Sh Regt
Earl C. Lowrie	Pvt	3206th QM Sv Co
Otto (NMI) Lutz Jr	Pvt	462d Amph Trk Co
Wilbert V. Lyon	Pvt	462d Amph Trk Co
Lawrence E. MacDonald	S/Sgt	3206th QM Sv Co
Patrick J. Mahoney	Pvt	3206th QM Sv Co
John (NMI) Mallassi	Pfc	3206th QM Sv Co
John V. Manak	Pfc	3206th QM Sv Co
Michael (NMI) Mance	Pvt	556th QM RH Co
Joseph P. Mancuso	T/5	478th Amph Trk Co
Robert E. Manes	Pvt	3206th QM Sv Co
Glenn R. Marcum	Pvt	557th QM RH Co
Joseph A. Marino	Pvt	557th QM RH Co
Patty (NMI) Marino	Pfc	557th QM RH Co
Ralph D. Marsh	Pfc	3206th QM Sv Co
Wilbur (NMI) Marts	Pfc	557th QM RH Co
Charles F. Massa	Pfc	478th Amph Trk Co
John I. Mathewson	Capt	Hq, 1st Engr Sp Brigade
Frank F. Mattos	T/5	462d Amph Trk Co
Haskel H. Mayfield	Pvt	3206th QM Sv Co
Louis B. McCampbell	Pfc	3206th QM Sv Co
Thomas B. McCormick	Sgt	607th QM GR Co
Roy E. McKinnon	T/5	3206th QM Sv Co
Earl M. McMore	T/5	462d Amph Trk Co
William F. Meehan	Pfc	3206th QM Sv Co
Robert H. Megathlin	T/5	462d Amph Trk Co
Trinidad (NMI) Mercado	T/5	462d Amph Trk Co
Paul A. Methner	Pfc	557th QM RH Co
Harry W. Mattler	Pvt	3206th QM Sv Co
Lawrence L. Meurer	Pfc	3206th QM Sv Co
Harry (NMI) Mieczkowski	T/5	33d Chem Decon Co
John A. Miglionico	T/5	478th Amph Trk Co
James E. Miller	Pvt	3206th QM Sv Co
James C. Mitchell	S/Sgt	557th QM RH Co
Albert (NMI) Mlaker	S/Sgt	478th Amph Trk Co
Norman C. Molander	Pfc	557th QM RH Co
Clarence (NMI) Monk	Pfc	557th QM RH Co
Robert C. Morang	Pfc	557th QM RH Co

Alvin G. Morgan	Pfc	3206th QM Sv Co
Aloysius G. Morgenstern	Pfc	557th QM RH Co
Edwin F. Morse	Pfc	557th QM RH Co
Robert P. Motley	Pvt	557th QM RH Co
Raymond J. Murphey	Cpl	557th QM RH Co
Hugh C. Murray	Pfc	3206th QM Sv Co
James E. Music	Pfc	557th QM RH Co
Michael J. Naccarelli	Pvt	462d Amph Trk Co
Curtis A. Nagle	Pfc	3206th QM Sv Co
Hyman (NMI) Nathan	Pvt	557th QM RH Co
Robert T. New	Pvt	3206th QM Sv Co
Aubrey L. Newman	Pfc	3206th QM Sv Co
Clarence C. Niedermeir	Sgt	607th QM GR Co
Joseph L. Noel	T/5	557th QM RH Co
Joseph (NMI) Occhipinti	Pvt	557th QM RH Co
Ubron M. Ogden	Pvt	462d Amph Trk Co
Michael A. Ogurek	Cpl	478th Amph Trk Co
John A. Olsen	Pfc	557th QM RH Co
Joseph L. Ostrowski	Pfc	462d Amph Trk Co
Lawrence W. Ott	Pfc	3206th QM Sv Co
Delbert E. Overton	Pvt	3206th QM Sv Co
Johnnie D. Owens	Pvt	3206th QM Sv Co
Helmer E. Panek	Pfc	33d Chem Decon Co
Frank (NMI) Parisi	Pfc	557th QM RH Co
Clifford F. Park	Pvt	531st Engr Sh Regt
James E. Park	Pvt	3206th QM Sv Co
Louis S. Patou	Pfc	625th Ord (AM) Co
Marvin L. Payton	Pvt	3206th QM Sv Co
Cleo B. Peake	Pfc	3206th QM Sv Co
Luther M. Pearson	Pvt	3206th QM Sv Co
Leray (NMI) Pemberton	Pvt	557th QM RH Co
Joe V. Penalver	Pvt	3206th QM Sv Co
Milton (NMI) Penn	Pfc	3206th QM Sv Co
Curtis (NMI) Pentecost	Pvt	556th QM RH Co
Gerrit (NMI) Peters	T/5	531st Engr Sh Regt
Lindsay (NMI) Peters Jr	2d Lt	3206th QM Sv Co
Charles R. Picking	Cpl	3206th QM Sv Co
Alfred E. Poggi	Cpl	3206th QM Sv Co
Edgar F. Pope	T/4	3206th QM Sv Co
Herrel K. Powell	1st Lt	478th Amph Trk Co
Clyde C. Pritchard	T/5	478th QM Sv Co
Isaac W. Pritt	Pfc	557th QM RH Co
Charles J. Pshenitzky	Pvt	3206th QM Sv Co
Thomas E. Raines	Pvt	3206th QM Sv Co
Ulton A. Ray	T/5	462d Amph Trk Co
Quirino A. Recchione	T/4	33d Chem Decon Co

William R. Reese	1/Sgt	3206th QM Sv Co
Thomas C. Reibel	Pvt	478th Amph Trk Co
Walter W. Reitzel	Pvt	3206th QM Sv Co
Lowell L. Renner	Pfc	3206th QM Sv Co
Irving (NMI) Rettinger	Pfc	3206th QM Sv Co
Alvin F. Richardson	Pvt	3206th QM Sv Co
Robert R. Riggs	Pfc	462d Amph Trk Co
James E. Roberson	Pvt	3206th QM Sv Co
Melvin A. Roberson	Pvt	3206th QM Sv Co
Lewis (NMI) Roberts	Pvt	557th QM RH Co
Ralph R. Roberts	Pvt	3206th QM Sv Co
Aristedes (NMI) Rodriguez	Pfc	3206th QM Sv Co
Tracy V. Rohrbaugh	Pfc	625th Ord (AM) Co
Rudolph J. Roper	Pvt	3206th QM Sv Co
Joseph A. Rosiek	Cpl	33d Chem Decon Co
Anthony J. Rosowski	Pvt	33d Chem Decon Co
Harry (NMI) Ruediger	T/5	462d Amph Trk Co
Victor P. Ruoto	Pvt	557th QM RH Co
Raymond G. Salemmo	Pfc	3206th QM Sv Co
Elmer J. Sanders	Pfc	697th QM GR Co
Harold L. Sanford	Pvt	3206th QM Sv Co
Edward T. Scanlon	T/5	478th Amph Trk Co
Richard C. Schleyer	Pvt	462d Amph Trk Co
Carl L. Schultheis	Pvt	462d Amph Trk Co
Stephen G. Schwartz	Pfc	557th QM RH Co
Conrad J. Schwechheimer	Pfc	557th QM RH Co
Ray E. Seibert	Capt	557th QM RH Co
Joseph H. Sessamen	Pvt	462d Amph Trk Co
Willard C. Sharff	Cpl	3206th QM Sv Co
John P. Sheahan Jr	Pfc	3206th QM Sv Co
James P. Sheridan	T/5	33d Chem Decon Co
Michael J. Shatkawski	Pfc	462d Amph Trk Co
Charles W. Sigman	Pvt	33d Chem Decon Co
Samuel (NMI) Silversmith	Pvt	557th QM RH Co
Leland (NMI) Simmons	Pfc	531st Engr Sh Regt
George R. Sitche	Pvt	3206th QM Sv Co
Steve L. Smerek	Cpl	3206th QM Sv Co
Jesse E. Smith	Pfc	625th Ord (AM) Co
Wallace W. Smith	Pfc	3206th QM Sv Co
Donald E. Snider	Pvt	462d Amph Trk Co
Wallace F. Snyder	Capt	3206th QM Sv Co
Herbert A. Southcott	T/5	478th Amph Trk Co
William F. Sparks	Pfc	3206th QM Sv Co
George E. Spitler	1/Sgt	33d Chem Decon Co
James W. Spurling	Pfc	3206th QM Sv Co
George W. Steen	Pvt	531st Angr Sh Regt

James W. Stephenson	Pfc	3206th QM Sv Co
Marshall L. Stevens	Pfc	531st Engr Sh Regt
Elmer D. Stillwell	T/5	607th QM GR Co
Horace A. Stokes	Pvt	33d Chem Decon Co
Glen T. Strader	Pvt	625th Ord (AM) Co
John W. Strapp	T/4	33d Chem Decon Co
Mathew E. Strubel	1st Lt	557th QM RH Co
Ralph A. Suesse	Capt	33d Chem Decon Co
Marvin L. Summerall	T/5	462d Amph Trk Co
Lennie C. Sutt	Pvt	3206th QM Sv Co
Richard E. Swanson	T/Sgt	1605th Engr Map Depot
Myles E. Sweeney	Pvt	557th QM RH Co
Owen A. Tate	Pfc	3206th QM Sv Co
Louis A. Tenuta	Pvt	3206th QM Sv Co
Joseph A. Tesoriero	Pvt	3206th QM Sv Co
Fay E. Thomas	Pfc	3206th QM Sv Co
Ernest M. Thompson	Pfc	607th QM GR Co
Mearl L. Toerber	Pfc	3206th QM Sv Co
John N. Tolie	Pfc	3206th QM Sv Co
Clarence H. Tomberlin	1st Lt	557th QM RH Co
Victor M. Torres	Cpl	3206th QM Sv Co
Joseph H. Tousignant	Pvt	531st Engr Sh Regt
Jacob (NMI) Trager	Pfc	3206th QM Sv Co
Stanley H. Treef	Pvt	3206th QM Sv Co
Luther R. Tucker	Pvt	3206th QM Sv Co
James L. Tuma Jr	1st Lt	557th QM RH Co
William A. Turk	Pvt	3206th QM Sv Co
Hillard (NMI) Tuttle	Pfc	531st Engr Sh Regt
Ernest (NMI) Tyson	Pvt	557th QM RH Co
Edward J. Unger	T/5	478th Amph Trk Co
Simon (NMI) Van Ess	T/5	462d Amph Trk Co
Clarence M. Van Nostrand	T/5	462d Amph Trk Co
John D. Veenbaas	Pvt	557th QM RH Co
Manuel (NMI) Vieira Jr	Pvt	557th QM RH Co
Richard F. Von Wald	S/Sgt	557th QM RH Co
Harold (NMI) Voorhees	Cpl	557th QM RH Co
Howard W. Wagner	Pvt	3206th QM Sv Co
Denver (NMI) Walker	Pfc	625th Ord (AM) Co
Joseph J. Walsh	T/3	1605th Engr Map Depot
Luther T. Ward	Pfc	607th QM GR Co
Gerald A. Watson	Pvt	3206th QM Sv Co
Grady D. Webb Jr	Pvt	531st Engr Sh Regt
Larry R. Wier	Pvt	607th QM GR Co
Emer O. Welch	T/5	478th Amph Trk Co
Chalcie G. West	Pvt	557th QM RH Co
Everett E. Whetstine	Pfc	3206th QM Sv Co

William L. Whitelock	Pvt	3206th QM Sv Co
Horace S. Williams	Cpl	3206th QM Sv Co
Obie D. Willis	T/4	557th QM Sv Co
Paul W. Wilson	Pfc	3206th QM Sv Co
Vernon S. Wilson	Pfc	3206th QM Sv Co
Floyd E. Wintjen	Pfc	3206th QM Sv Co
Russel L. Wirt	Pvt	3206th QM Sv Co
Henry F. Wolfgram	T/5	462d Amph Trk Co
Frederick J. Wolpert	Pvt	3206th QM Sv Co
Stanley K. Wood	Pfc	33d Chem Decon Co
Darryl V. Wooderson	Pfc	3206th QM Sv Co
Joseph O. Wright	Pvt	557th QM RH Co
Myron A. Wright Jr	Pfc	3206th QM Sv Co
John E. Wyckoff	Pfc	462d Amph Trk Co
Mike J. Yadrick	Pfc	3206th QM Sv Co
Dominick (NMI) Yangrello	Pvt	557th QM RH Co
John W. Yates	Sgt	3206th QM Sv Co
Lawrence C. Zemple	Pfc	557th QM RH Co

NAVY CASUALTIES – DEAD AND MISSING

USS LST 507

Dead

Lieut. J. S. Swarts, USNR
Lieut. Kennan H. Smith, USNR
Lieut. (jg) Henry Q. Saucier, USNR
Lieut. (jg) Bruce B. Hofman, USNR
Ensign James J. Clark, USNR
Ensign Conner D. Collins, Jr., USNR

Bailey, James (n)	Y2c
Bennen, Charles D.	BM2c
Blackie, Henry A.	S2c
Del Duca, Thomas J., Jr.	Cox
Bettencourt, John J.	MoMM3c
Cusack, Vincent P.	S2c
Cleary, James F.	HA2c
Crowe, James T., Jr.	MoMM2c
Dickerson, William W.	SK2c
Dailey, Carl W.	PhM2c
Dinneen, Joseph M.	BM1c
Dobson, Henry R.	PhM2c
Durrum, James W.	S1c
Eisenbach, Harold E.	SC2c
Field, Paul R.	QM3c
Fitts, Felton T.	GM2c
Gambrel, Jake (n)	S2c
Garlock, Charles W.	QM2c
Griffen, Jimmie W.	SC3c
Gibson, Richard M.	S1c
Goldsmith, Leonard (n)	S2c
Gulledge, William T.	S2c
Grecco, Joseph G.	S1c
Grehan, Raymond R.	GM3c

Hoffman, Russell W.	S1c
Hampton, Jerry P.	S2c
King, Philip E.	F2c
Karasinski, Louis F.	S1c
Koski, Theodore J.	MoMM2c
Ledbetter, Alvin L.	S2c
Martin, Howard A.	S2c
Maggard, Daniel W., Jr.	S2c
Moore, Joseph M.	S2c
Morancy, Edgar F.	S2c
Mackey, Robert C.	Cox
Miller, John H.	S2c
Meyers, Lester A.	F2c
Mathews, John E.	S2c
Malott, Robert J.	PhM3c
O'Connell, Michael J.	MoMM2c
Ryan, James P., Jr.	SM3c
Raptis, Charles G.	PhM3c
Ragusa. Paul M.	PhM3c
Rogers, William L.	Ha2c
Sutherland, Pete J.	S2c
Schreiber, William H.	S2c
Stanesic. John L.	HA2c
Staudt, Charles J., Jr.	MoMM1c
Sullivan, George A.	S2c
Squiers, Lawrence P.	MoMM2c
Woods, Deward W.	GM1c
Wright, Curtis M.	Ha2c

Missing

Burns, Sylvester M.	EM3c
Carroll, Francis A.	MoMM2c
Grunther, Nelson (n)	SM3c
Lighty, Frank T.	MoMM3c
Sturdivant, Malcolm E.	WT2c
Watson, Andrew (n)	MoMM1c
Whipple, Frank L.	S2c
Weinbrot, Harold M.	HA1c
Ricketts, Richard E.	HA2c
Scott, Kenneth L.	HA2c
Saxton, Robert E.	HA2c
Trgovic, Steve J.	HA2c
Tully, Joseph E.	HA2c

USS LST 531

Dead

Lieut. L. H. Levy, USNR
Lieut. (jg) John H. Hill, USNR
Lieut. (jg) Tiffany V. Manning USNR
Ensign Walter P. Jackman, USNR
Ensign J. J. Gallaher, USNR

Achey, Allen O., Jr.	MoMM3c
Brock, Norris G.	S1c
Baugher, Ellis W.	HA2c
Bolling, Floyd H.	S2c
Benton, Elmer C	S2c
Coyle, Michael J.	Bkr3c
Callas, Vincent M.	S1c
Cowan, Eugene R.	S1c
Carr, Frederick C.	Cox
Denton, Harold C.	SM3c
Dawson, Glenn H.	HA2c
Edson, Richard W.	S2c
Hauber, Bernard A.	EM2c
Hayth, Eugene (n)	SF2c
Harrell, Charles (n)	HA1c
Holmes, Samuel D.	MoMM2c
Hurley, James W.	HA2c
Jacques, Edmond L.	S2c

Kessinger, Mark F. S2c
Kuhns, Harold D. S2c
Kirkwood, Ralph A. F2c
Krizanosky, Alexander (n) F2c
Kelley, Ford H. S2c
Land, Charles G. S2c
Leeman, Hollace H. HA2c
Lacey, Burvil E. S2c
Locklear, Melvin L. CCS(AA)
Levine, Harry (n) HA1c
Miller, Ralph R. Cox
Montgomery, Doyle D. Y1c
Peters, James D. Cox
Pear, Williams (n) EM3c
Parker, Cornelius J. MoMM2c
Petcavage, William J. S1c
Sheppard, Thanuel V. GM3c
Sochaki, Edward A. PhM2c
Schimanske, Daniel R. GM3c
Solomon, William (n) HA1c
Stemats, Steve J. RM3c
Showers, Lyle F. PhM3c
Unger, Alvin C. SK3c
Vandeland, Albert J. S1c
Witten, Lloyd L. CPhM
Waugh, James N. S1c

Missing

Lieut. J. W. M. Behrens, USN
Ensign A. F. Cram, USNR
Ensign L. O. Nelson, USNR
Ensign W. H. Cantrell, USNR

Bliss, Arthur H. S2c
Bridgham, Wade L. QM3c
Brummitt, Clifton H., Jr. S1c
Cobern, William W. MoMM3c
Colwell, Richard L. S2c
Croswell, Curtis W. S1c
Cruz, Joseph (n), Jr. MoMM3c
Czerwinski William J. F1c
Danley, Harry I. S1c
Degouff, Theodore D. S1c
Dobson, Edwin J. S2c
Duffy, Ralph O'C GM1c
Fisher, 'K' 'C' StM2c
Ford, Hobart (n). Jr. GM2c
Gaboys, Edward A. S1c
Gurn, Murray B. PhM2c
Hartman, Robert J. EM3c
Hopkins, Lawrence E. S2c
Jencovic, Albert J. S2c
Johnson, Albert W., Jr. EM3c
Kartz, Henry (n) EM2c
Kerby, Reuben G. S2c
Kirby, Grady E. S2c
Marcus, Emery E., Jr. SC3c
McGuen, Frank A. MoMM1c
McLean, Robert W. MoMM2c
Noble, Elisha G. StM2c
Peterson, Robert D. F2c
Phillips, Kenneth F2c
Pogue, Richard (n) F2c

Shea, John Maurice	QM3c
Shengarn, George (n)	MoMM3c
Spangler, Walter A.	Cox
Taylor, George W.	S2c
Townsend, Wille W.	StM2c
Walls, James W.	S2c
Walters Robert G.	S2c
Watsch, Raleigh F.	S2c
White, Earnest T.	EM3c
Borgerson, Ray (n)	GM3c
Brickey, William E.	Cox
Christoffel, Raymond J.	S1c
Ellis, John J.	S1c
Scott, James O.	MM2c
Starr, Joseph L., Jr.	MM2c
Drake, Robert G.	Cox
Corideo, Richard V.	S1c
Debias, Edward G.	Cox
Cason, Paskel O.	S1c
Anderson, Williard C.	S1c
Kaska, Albert P.	S1c
Jansen, Melvin J.	S1c
Cummings, Eugene F.	MoMM2c
Poloncarz, John E.	S1c
Hall, William C.	PhM3c
Goldstein, Samuel (n)	HA1c
Merrill, William J.	HA2c
Neal, Kermit H.	HA2c
Ruguai, Daniel L.	HA2c
Samuelson, Gail E.	HA2c
Stoklosa, Edward	HA2c

USS LST 289

Dead

Griffin, Joseph W.	SK2c
Muza, Earl V.	S2c
Neff, Harold A.	S2c
Roberts, Clifford L.	QM3c
Shipp, John L., Jr.	S1c
Broske, Mitchel L.	GM3c
Chandler, James W.	GM2c
Hackes, Mike G.	S2c
Harvie, James H.	S2c
Kortenhorn, Herman R.	F1c
May, Robert M.	S2c

Missing

Frazier, Walter H.	S2c
Muller, William C.	S2c

INDEX